VILLAGE

Life

ANGELA CORRELL

TEN PEAKS PRESS®
EUGENE, OR

The quote of Paul the apostle (chapter 5) is from Romans 12:13.

The quote of Paul the apostle (chapter 15) is from 1 Thessalonians 4:11.

The quote of the prophet Moses (chapter 20) is from Leviticus 23:2-3.

All Scripture verses are taken from the ESV® Bible (The Holy Bible, English Standard Version®), copyright © 2001 by Crossway, a publishing ministry of Good News Publishers. Used with permission. All rights reserved. The ESV text may not be quoted in any publication made available to the public by a Creative Commons license. The ESV may not be translated in whole or in part into any other language.

Author is represented by Jenni Burke of Illuminate Literary Agency: www.illuminateliterary.com

Cover design by Faceout Studio, Spencer Fuller

Interior design by Faceout Studio, Paul Nielsen

Photos on pages 6, 8, 11, 18, 24, 46, 62, 64, 98, 101, 108, 121, 140, 164, 166, 169, 170, 173, 174, 176, 179, 180, 183, 196, 199, 200, 210 by 6PM STUDIO SRLS, www.6pmstudio.com; photos on pages 56, 112, 114, 117, 118, 122, 152, 194, 204 by Gabe Osborne; photos on pages 28 (bottom), 38, 142, 209, 224 by Baldini/Bruzaite, www.medisproject.com; photo on page 203 by John O'Malley.

Cover photos and all other photos by Jason Asa McKinley.

Illustrations © Viktoriia Zavodnytska / Shutterstock; © twinstudio / Shutterstock; © mushan / Shutterstock; © Dendy Harya / Shutterstock; © W. Phokin / Shutterstock; © Christos Georghiou / Shutterstock

For bulk or special sales, please call 1-800-547-8979. Email: CustomerService@hhpbooks.com

TEN PEAKS PRESS is a federally registered trademark of The Hawkins Children's LLC. Harvest House Publishers, Inc., is the exclusive licensee of this trademark.

Neither the author nor publisher is responsible for any outcome from use of the recipes in this book. The recipes are intended for informational purposes and those who have the appropriate culinary skills. USDA guidelines should always be followed in food preparation. The author and publisher make no warranty, express or implied, in any recipe.

Village Life

Published by Ten Peaks Press, an imprint of Harvest House Publishers

Eugene, Oregon 97408

ISBN 978-0-7369-8844-5 (hardcover)

ISBN 978-0-7369-8845-2 (eBook)

Library of Congress Control Number: 2024952306

Printed in China

25 26 27 28 29 30 31 32 33 / RDS / 10 9 8 7 6 5 4 3 2 1

To Jess,

always

Contents

Introduction

During our times in Tuscany these past eleven years, I've met so many people who were drawn to the Italian countryside by some deep, inner need for connection. A connection to art, beauty, craftsmanship, creation, a slower pace, a nurturing meal, a rhythmic period of rest, and long walks in nature.

These often provide a path to deeper connections with others and with God. Tuscany gives us a chance to reimagine our lives, infused with lessons from an ancient culture. This desire for connection and redirection is part of my own story, recounted in Restored in Tuscany: Facing Loss, Finding Beauty, and Living Forward in Hope.

My husband, Jess, and I took our small-town rural Southern roots into this adventure. We are both seventh-generation Kentuckians; our ancestors carved their way into the wilderness before it was even a state. Neither of us has ever lived outside of a fifty-mile radius from the place of our birth. And yet here we find ourselves, with feet and heart in both, claiming citizenship in a place we can only describe as Kentuscany.

A village is defined as a cluster of homes forming a small community, often surrounded by countryside. This rural influence is both familiar and attractive to us. In the past few years, as part-time hilltop dwellers of a tiny medieval village, we have discovered even more similarities to Kentucky that made this Tuscan community feel like home, along with a treasure trove of differences that delight, amuse, and inspire.

While we connect deeply with the agricultural aspects after decades of farm living, it is a new experience for us to be in close community with our Italian friends and neighbors. So many things are shared in this place, from walls to cats to the tiny road, and respectful behavior is necessary to live in harmony with other people in a small space. There is a natural rhythm of life in this ancient village, days to weeks to seasons, rooted centuries back into Etruscan culture and infused by the Sardinian immigrants.

Through this experience on an enchanted Italian hilltop, my hope is to share this with you through observations, stories, photographs, recipes, and ideas, so you, too, may enjoy a bit of Tuscan village life in your own neck of the woods, wherever it may be.

1

Vicino

{NEAR OR NEIGHBOR}

Surely heaven must have something of the color and shape of whatever
village or hill or cottage of which the believer says, This is my own.
—WILLIAM FAULKNER

O ur adopted Tuscan village, like so many medieval villages, has a long and rich history. It began in the 1200s with a settlement of Cistercian monks below the hill who built an abbey and were known as *fullones*, Latin for those who worked and washed wool, using the water of the nearby stream. As time went by, the ground supporting a section of their abbey became unstable and it began to collapse. The abbey's demise impacted the water course, making the settlement's location even more fragile. The monks and the population around the abbey decided to leave the area and climbed up the mountain—hence the name, Mount Fullones, those who work wool, or Monte Follonico, now combined into one word, Montefollonico. The village coat of arms includes an image of the wool clothing, a reminder of the origins.

A wall was constructed around the village hilltop and eventually included seven fortified towers and three entrance gates. Later, the strategic position made the village a valuable outpost for Siena against the village of Montepulciano, an ally of Florence, during the great rivalry between Florence and Siena.

The village sits astride a ridgetop with the Val d'Orcia on one side and the Val di Chiana on the other, looking like a great warship keeping watch over both valleys, a small but mighty guardian. Hilltop outposts are naturally away from springs, creeks, and rivers, so water is captured in great cisterns for drinking, but also for washing and cleaning. Even today, we funnel rain water in our backyard cistern so we can keep our flowers and plants alive during the long and dry months of summer.

Cultural and architectural holdovers from the founding of the village are both practical and curious. Medieval-style defenses are still in use through shutters and iron bars designed to protect from unwanted intruders. Heavy wooden doors, iron latches, towers, and the double entrance gates for extra fortification remind us of how villagers lived under the threat of invasion long ago.

The medieval-style door on our house serves a practical purpose when we're in Italy. Jess opens the outer door each morning, eager to see what's happening outside our doorstep. Has Luciana made it to the pharmacy? Is Antonio polishing his motorcycle in preparation for a ride? Are the cooking schools on their way to a class? Our quiet one-car street has a surprising amount of activity if you are watching.

When I'm there alone, I usually leave the outer door closed until I'm finished writing and out of my pajamas. Once the door is open, it's a signal to friends we're ready for visitors. In a small village, people often stop by your door to exchange some information, drop something off, or even just to say hello. It's the advantage of living in proximity. There's no need for the formality of an appointment, although sometimes one is arranged.

On warm days, I often open my kitchen door and let the breeze come freely through the screen. From there, I see the back porch of Fausto and Viviana, our elderly but fit and feisty neighbors, and I check to see if they have opened their doors. Fausto usually comes out in his pajamas to feed the cat, a fat little calico who sits on Fausto's porch and waits to see which of us will open the door first. If it's me, she dashes over with surprising agility for a petite feline with an overly plump frame. She then leaps to my doorstep, ready for the milk I pour into her bowl. Sometimes, she comes to the back door in my writing room and asks to come in for a bit. I call her Pina, since Fausto claims she has no name and is not his cat. He may think she doesn't belong to him, but I've seen him with the cat curled against his chest as he

leans back in his chair, soaking up the summer-morning sun. Later, after our original exchange on her name, or lack of it, I learned Fausto started calling her Capina, just at the time I decided she was Pina.

Cats are everywhere in Montefollonico, sitting on windowsills, skittering across the narrow streets, and stretching lazily on benches in the morning sun. Cats are welcome and serve to manage the rodent population in historic villages, although some villagers place water bottles by the door stoops to keep them from leaving certain unwanted gifts. The reflection in the water is supposed to scare them away, but Pina has no worries here. Fausto and I are rolling out the welcome mat.

✦

Many villagers tend their plants like beloved pets. The bright red and pink geraniums, petunias, and sedums flow over terra-cotta pots, while the climbing jasmine lends a delicate fragrance to the breeze, and the plants give texture and color to the stone walls.

An early-morning walk through the village, as golden sunlight slants across honey-colored stone, lends the comforting sounds of clicking latches as doors and shutters open, the trickle of water as plants and cats are given a morning drink, and the gentle exchanges between neighbors.

Then, of course, there are morning grocery trips to the *alimentari*, managed efficiently by the mother and two daughters who run the shop and parish activities, all while cooking ready-to-eat meals and supplying daily bread and provisions for the village.

The other village spot to connect with locals is the Bar Sport, for morning coffees and pastries, daytime sandwiches, and evening *aperitivi*. The Italian bar is very different than the American idea of a bar, and while there is certainly alcohol available—and sometimes liqueur is used in coffee to make a *caffè corretto*, or a corrected coffee—it is always a coffee shop complete with barista and open to all generations.

Depending on the time of day, a cappuccino and a *cornetto con crema*, a delicious croissant filled with yellow cream, can be just the antidote after a long spell of traveling. Sipping on a frothy drink and taking in the view of Monte Amiata across the Val d'Orcia reminds my jet-lagged body of exactly where we are.

As lunch approaches, everyone disappears into their homes for midday sustenance only to emerge after the rest period is over.

During late afternoons, the elders take seats on the stone bench at the town gate and watch village comings and goings. The early evening is the time of *la passeggiata,* the stroll before dinner, when many villagers walk about and greet their neighbor, or sit at the bar for an *aperitivo.* It's a time to watch, to visit, to relax.

In the evenings, and especially on weekends, the bar becomes the social gathering place, spilling out of the small space and into a gravel garden with plastic chairs and tables for seating. Once, I watched the locals pass a television through the bar window so it could be placed on an outside table allowing for a larger crowd to watch a famous soccer match. At other times, summer weekends at the bar might feature live music, filling the street nearby with melodic sounds and drawing in those who want to talk, laugh, and even dance.

While this village is living and breathing, and in every way a slice of real life in Tuscany, it cannot escape the dreamlike mirage it often presents with a glance off the hilltop toward the Val d'Orcia or the Val di Chiana, or during an evening stroll through the streets when the sun warms the village stones and enhances the beauty of the wheat fields in the valley floor below.

The blooming flowers and climbing plants, the musical notes of Italian conversation, and sometimes the scent of sizzling garlic near lunchtime, wafting down from an upstairs kitchen, remind us we are back in this place, even though it often seems a distant dream. With this reminder, Jess throws open our medieval-style wooden doors.

We are at home in Tuscany.

Bring Italy Home

- ⚜ Invite your neighbors over for a morning coffee, Italian style, perhaps featuring some pastries along with plum or fig jam. For tips on how to create a real Italian cappuccino, check out the recipe.

- ⚜ Read *Restored in Tuscany: A True Story of Facing Loss, Finding Beauty, and Living Forward in Hope* for our backstory.

- ⚜ Cappuccino maker recommendation: After trying out several machines, my personal favorite is the De'Longhi La Specialista. This is a good value for a cappuccino maker, combining the right mix of manual options and automation for those of us wanting an in-home cappuccino machine.

Un pecorino mondiale
Premiato in Norvegia

Cappuccino

While American gas stations have promoted the idea of a cappuccino with flavored powdered milk laden with sugar, and coffee shops offer pumps of sugary flavored syrups, the real Italian cappuccino is something quite different.

There is an art to making a good cappuccino, and plenty of opinions on the ratio between foam and coffee, amount of the espresso, and roasting style of the beans. Espresso machines can cost anywhere from a few hundred dollars to several thousand dollars, and they vary widely between manual and automated. Most Italians use the moka pot to make their in-home espressos. These work like small stovetop percolators and are inexpensive. There are also handheld milk frothers to foam the milk, which enables you to have a budget-friendly cappuccino.

However you decide to go about your cappuccino, here is a basic recipe, using a machine like the De'Longhi.

INGREDIENTS

Espresso roast coffee beans   **Fresh, cold whole milk**

DIRECTIONS

Pour your espresso beans into the grinder. Finely grind the beans into the filter basket. Use the tamper to press the ground coffee into the basket.

Attach the filter basket to the machine and lock it into place. Press the button so the hot water will flow through the coffee and into the cup (make sure to select the right setting for an espresso). This is called "pulling the espresso shot."

Pour the cold milk into a stainless-steel frothing cup. Release a bit of steam from the wand to get rid of any excess water, then lower the tip into the milk, beginning just below the surface to froth. As the volume increases and the frothing cup warms up, lower the wand into the cup at an angle, creating a little whirlpool inside the cup. Turn off the steamer and remove the wand. Swirl the steamed milk and foam, then pour it on top of the espresso. A good rule of thumb is equal parts of coffee, steamed milk, and foamed milk, but create your own to taste.

2

Saluti

{GREETINGS}

Buongiorno, the morning greeting is a caress from afar to your heart.
—UNKNOWN

*C*iao, y'all, or *Ciao*-dy! The way we greet one another is rooted deep within our heritage. Because Jess and I were raised in rural Southern towns, it's natural for us to greet most everyone in some fashion, even when passing on the street. It would be rude not to make eye contact and at least give a nod of greeting, a polite hello, or a "good morning."

It's with this cultural background that we booked a first-time two-week stay in a small Tuscan village. Jess had grasped the term *ciao*, a word that means hello and goodbye in Italian, but we didn't yet realize it is meant to be used for people you know. Since any other greeting was more difficult to pronounce, Jess *ciao*'d everyone we passed, in his big, friendly American way. The responses ranged from startled to a flat-out open-mouthed stare.

Over the years, we have learned how to properly greet our neighbors, friends, and strangers. *Buongiorno* for the morning. After lunch, we switch to *buona sera*, and when leaving a restaurant or a friend's house after dinner, we say *buona notte*. The more old-fashioned *salve* works anytime as a polite greeting. It goes back historically to the ancient Romans, who used to greet one another with a wish for good health by using this word. Now it has evolved to a more general greeting, but it has a lovely wish behind it. If exiting a shop or a place where we have just met someone, we say goodbye with the more formal *arrivederci* instead of *ciao*.

Somehow, this grasp of the polite Italian greetings has also transferred to my own way of greeting friends and neighbors in my American town. I say "good morning" much more often than I used to, either in person or on email or text, rather than rushing headlong into business. I also regularly use "good afternoon," "good evening," and even "good night."

We've learned when meeting someone in Italy for the first time, it's fine to simply acknowledge the person with a smile while making eye contact—shake hands if you like, but the nice thing to say is *piacere*, or "pleased," which is short for "pleased to meet you." These are simple words but go a long way in initial greetings.

Friends or family in Italy often greet one another with air kisses. In my early days, this created a bit of anxiety because I never knew which side to go to first and ended up face dancing with the other person. To make it even more confusing, if you look up Italian kisses, it says to kiss on the left. But to kiss on the left cheek, you must lean to the right. So, right is left. Or left is right.

⁂

It's common for many of us to greet someone and ask how they are without really expecting an honest response. We often respond with "Fine, thank you," even when our world is falling apart. Not so in a small Tuscan village.

If you venture beyond "good morning" and ask, "How are you?" in Italian, be prepared. You are likely to get a very honest answer. I have been told about eye problems and bunions—and everything in between. I have also asked someone who has recently lost a loved one how they are doing, and they answered honestly, "I am not doing well." Sometimes, it's hard to know what to say in response, especially with limited Italian, yet the conversation is never left there. At the end, the villager will shrug and say, "*È la vita*. It's life."

There is truth in this statement. This is the life we all lead, we humans in a broken world, facing physical and emotional pain, and it's refreshing to

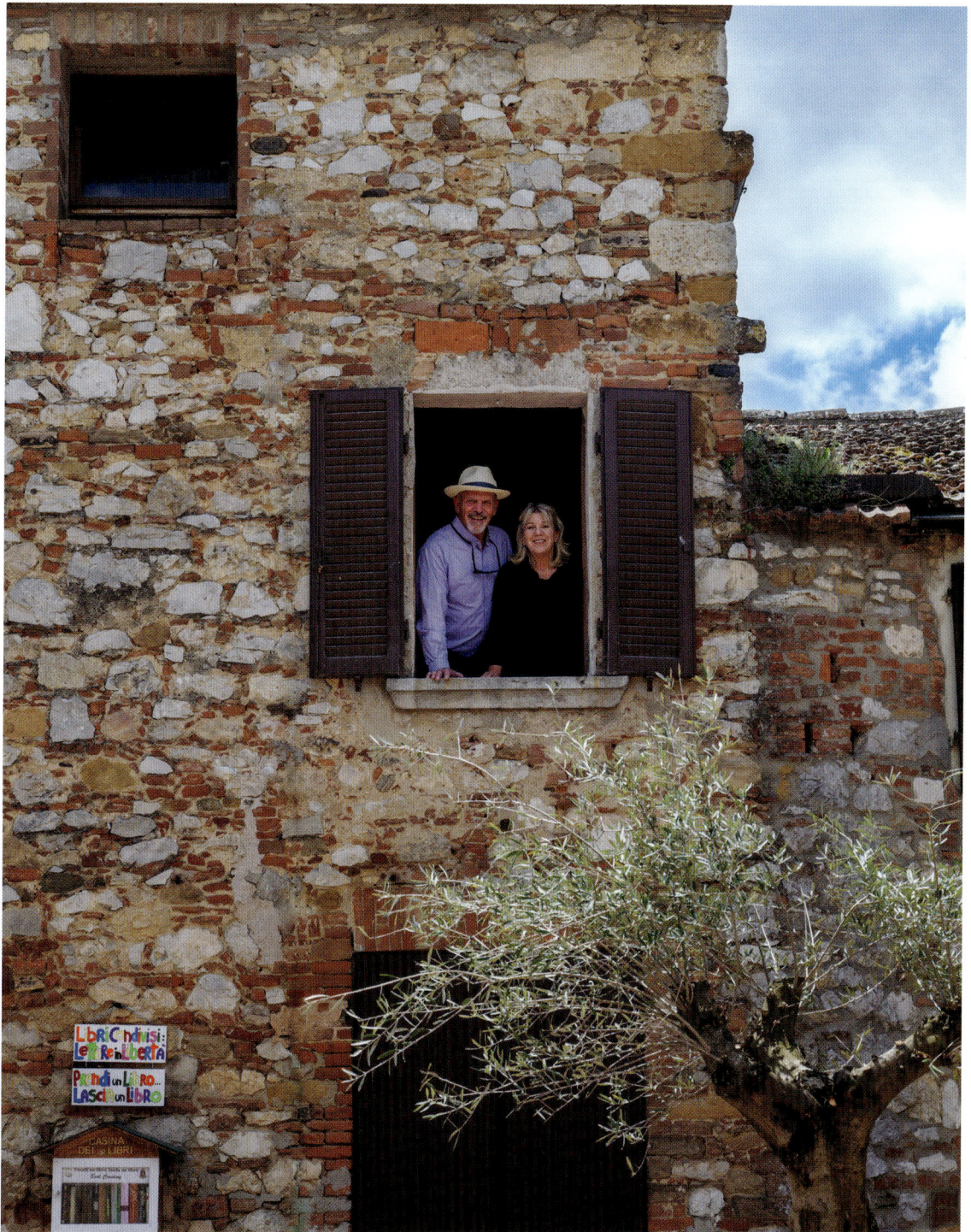

openly acknowledge this fact rather than saying all is well when it's not.

Another informal greeting I have often heard in the village is *ecco* (then someone's name). It just means "here's so-and-so," but it's often delivered in an exuberant voice, showing pleasure.

One of my favorite greetings to hear is *bentornati!* This is the plural form of "welcome back" and is often the greeting we receive after being away for weeks or months.

⬥

Every year, usually in December, a festival is held in our village to judge the best *vin santo* makers. Vin santo translates to "holy wine" and is made from dried grapes, so the sugar is concentrated. It is a sweet dessert wine, taken after dinner, and often served with *cantucci* (cookies) to be dipped into the wine as a sweet and crunchy ending to the meal. Hopeful contestants from various neighboring towns and villages submit their creations, and the wine is judged numerically in order from the best to the last. There is a particular greeting associated with this festival: *"Lo gradireste un goccio di vin santo? Would you like a drop of vin santo?"*

While you may not be able to attend the vin santo festival, let me at least welcome you, *benvenuti*. Join me on this discovery journey about Tuscan village life—and please, settle in with a drop of vin santo if you like.

Bring Italy Home

⚜ Sprinkle polite greetings throughout your daily conversation, texts, and emails.

⚜ Read *I Promessi Sposi*, or *The Betrothed*, a classic Italian historical novel.

⚜ Watch the movie *Enchanted April*.

⚜ Listen to the Italian songs of Dean Martin, Frank Sinatra, and Perry Como.

Cantucci

Siriana Fumi teaches a master class for Tuscan Women Cook, a cooking school based in Montefollonico, and her cantucci is a favorite. Cantucci is a Tuscan almond *biscotti* (meaning "twice cooked"). Cantucci is traditionally served with vin santo and dipped into the drink for a delightfully sweet and crunchy dessert.

You can make these using all-purpose flour, but blending in cake flour produces a better result. If toasting your own almonds, preheat the oven to 325°. Line a rimmed baking sheet with parchment paper or foil for easy cleanup. Roast for 10 to 15 minutes.

INGREDIENTS

3¼ cups all-purpose flour
¾ cup cake flour
1½ cups granulated sugar
2½ tsp. baking powder
4 whole eggs

2 large egg yolks
Grated zest of 1 whole orange
Grated zest of 1 whole lemon
7 oz. toasted almonds
Egg wash: 1 whole egg, lightly beaten

DIRECTIONS

Preheat the oven to 350°F. Line a baking sheet with parchment paper.

Stir together the flours, sugar, and baking powder in a large bowl. Transfer the mixture to a flat worktable. Make a well in the center. Pour the whole eggs, egg yolks, and zest into the well. Knead the mixture using your hands until it starts to come together. If the dough feels dry, add an additional egg yolk or whole egg. Add the whole toasted almonds and knead until you have a firm and flexible dough. This can also be done in a stand mixer using the dough hook.

Divide the dough into two even pieces. Roll each piece into a log approximately 2 inches wide. Place them on the parchment-paper-lined baking sheet. Brush each log lightly with the egg wash.

Bake until the dough is slightly golden, for about 30 to 35 minutes. Remove the baked logs from the oven. Let them cool for 15 minutes. Then place them on a cutting board. Cut the logs on the diagonal approximately ½ inch thick. If you prefer firmer cookies, return the cut slices to the oven. Reduce the heat to 325°F and bake them for 8 to 10 additional minutes.

Recipe courtesy of Tuscan Women Cook

YIELD: 48 cookies

3

Il Tempo

{TIME}

It takes a man of genius to travel in his own country, in his native village; to make any progress between his door and his gate.

—HENRY DAVID THOREAU

Chi va piano va sano e lontano.
He who goes slowly goes healthy and far.

—ITALIAN PROVERB

"*Domani mattina,*" the mechanic said. Tomorrow morning.

"*Si, quando?* Yes, when?" In other words, I asked exactly what time we can bring the car.

"*Domani mattina,*" he said again, shrugging his shoulders. He added, "*Dieci o undici.*" Ten or eleven—as if he were spelling something out to a child. I am not the only one who has struggled to pin down exact times in Italy. An expat friend once tried to clarify the time for a meeting set as *dopo cena,* or after dinner. "What time after dinner?"

The Italian answered, "Nine or nine fifteen, whenever everyone is done with dinner." Naturally. This fluidity of time can be rather unnerving for many folks, but once adjusted, it's also liberating.

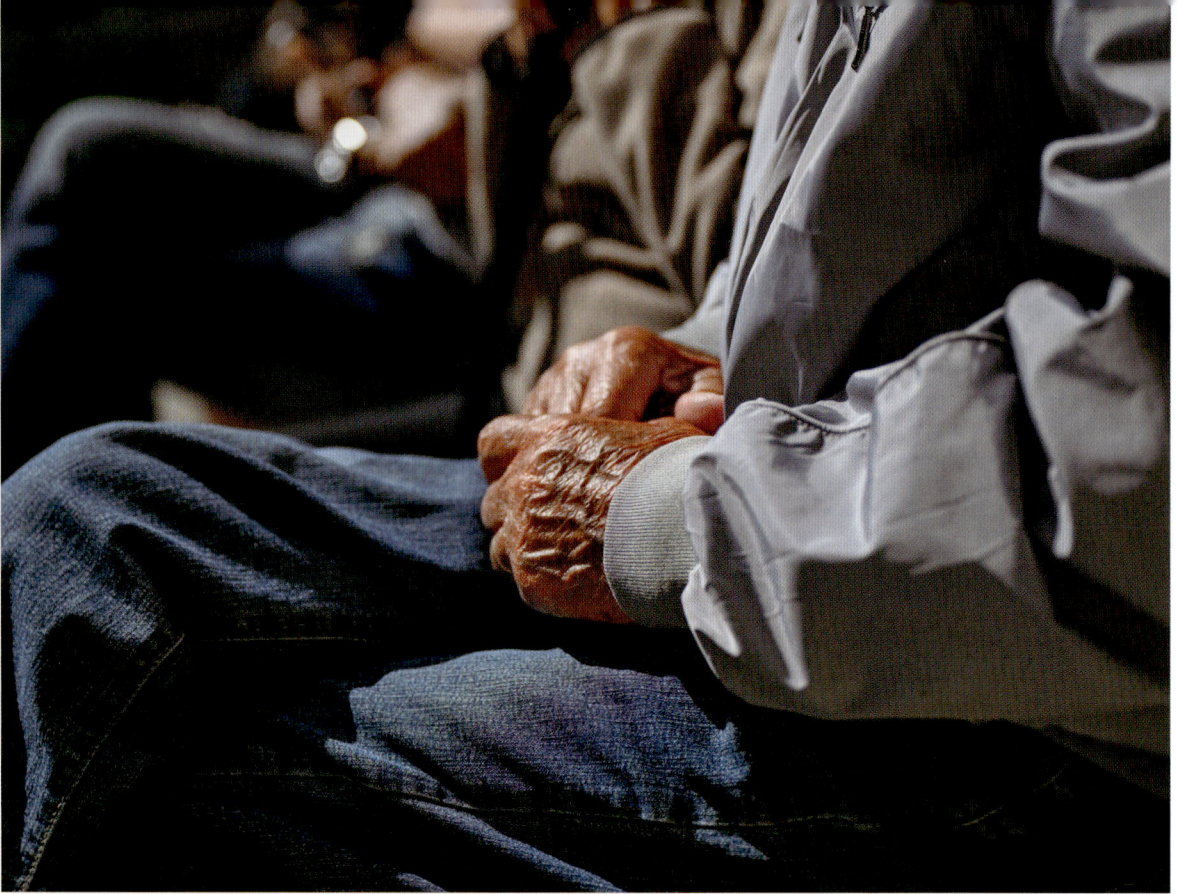

Beyond appointments, even getting from one place to another or accomplishing one small task could possibly take hours, as we have learned repeatedly.

One day, Jess and I set out to do one small job. We needed to move an old grandfather clock from the cantina of a neighboring property to the upstairs so it could be taken to a restorer.

As we were entering the building, neighbors called out to us from the upstairs window of the house next door. We greeted them and they asked about Jess's painting, since he had been using the empty space as a temporary studio. He showed them his latest painting, and then the wife said her husband was also a painter. He had a studio inside their house—would we like to see?

We looked at each other with only slight hesitation. The errand could wait, but these invitations are golden. Up we went to the third floor of the palazzo where their apartment is located. We toured their living quarters, admired his studio, his artwork, his father's artwork, and the stunning views from their unique position at the edge of the village. After the tour, we were invited to sit at the table where a bottle of prosecco was produced, along with some crackers. We learned where they were born, where they lived most of their lives, who they were related to in the village, when they married, how many children they have, and when they began their retirement. We took our leave only after sharing our contact information so we could make plans to spend more time together.

This type of encounter has happened countless times in our village—a walk down the street that results in a tour of someone's home or a visit at their kitchen table. These experiences were not common when we were tourists, but now that we are a part of the village, we have been given membership as *montanini*, a moniker for inhabitants of Montefollonico.

We have learned to plan extra time for any errands or tasks, such as going to the alimentari for groceries, even though the shop is a mere hundred yards away. On that short walk, it's possible to stop and have multiple conversations on the way, not to mention the conversations inside the market. Sometimes these chats lead to invitations or plans for a more extensive visit, such as coffee at the bar or a glass of wine in the evening.

When Jess disappeared recently right before dinner to pick up olive oil from our neighbor down the street, he was gone for an hour. I looked out the front door to find him chatting with neighbors in the middle of the street.

The same can happen walking to the car. When I have an appointment in a neighboring village, I must plan not only for the time it takes to walk to my car parked outside the village but also for the time I will stop and chat on the way. Margin is essential and offers the opportunity to cultivate the art of lingering and savoring, two beautiful gifts.

Bring Italy Home

- ❖ Give yourself an extra fifteen minutes before every appointment to leave space for unexpected interruptions.

- ❖ Cultivate the art of lingering a few extra minutes over meals and in conversation.

- ❖ Read the book *A Room with a View* by E.M. Forster.

- ❖ Explore films by Federico Fellini, most famous for *La Dolce Vita*.

Bruschetta Pomodoro

(pronounced *broo-skeh-tuh* in Italian)

INGREDIENTS

1 lb. fresh Roma tomatoes
1 tsp. sea salt, divided
Small to medium loaf of crusty bread,
  sliced

Garlic clove
10 to 12 basil leaves, divided
4 T. extra-virgin olive oil

DIRECTIONS

Chop the tomatoes and put in a colander. Sprinkle some of the sea salt over them and stir, then allow the tomatoes to drain for 30 minutes to an hour. Grill or toast the bread and rub with a peeled garlic clove.

    Slice six large basil leaves. Put the drained tomatoes in a bowl and add the basil, olive oil, and remaining salt. Toss together and spread atop the bread slices, saving the remaining basil leaves for garnish.

YIELD: **8 servings**

4

Connessione

{CONNECTION}

If you talk to a man in a language he understands, that goes to his head. If you talk to him in his language, that goes to his heart.
—NELSON MANDELA

A different language is a different vision of life.
—FEDERICO FELLINI

There was a time when I ordered mattresses for our house in Tuscany before realizing we were in for a yearlong renovation. The mattress store owner patiently stored the mattresses, and one day I sent a message to him saying I would "touch base soon about the mattresses."

"Angela, I am sorry. What this mean, touch base?"

I was surprised to realize I had carelessly used an American baseball metaphor to communicate with an Italian who was using a translator app. This drove home how often my speech is infused with metaphors and similes, expressions meaningless in a different culture.

Not only has it been a challenge to drop the metaphors, it's also been a challenge to pronounce entire words, since Southerners so often trail off the end of the word, leaving the last letter or so to the imagination. Despite all these challenges, Jess and I are conscious of the need to learn more of the language so we can communicate on a deeper level with our Italian friends. Learning the language is the only path to meaningful relationships. *Piano, piano,* as the Italians say. Slowly, slowly.

⸙

Around the time I started learning Italian, I went to my local Walmart one day to buy some jars, lids, and bands for summer garden canning. A farmer in overalls sat near the exit on a bench. As I rolled by, he looked at my full cart and asked, "Wha ye gonna can?" I answered immediately, "Green beans!" He smiled back in approval. This short conversation made me imagine how hard it would be to understand for an Italian learning English. I'm not even sure someone from Michigan would have understood.

We face a similar challenge with all the proverbs, metaphors, accents, and dialects of Italian. Currently, my skills are enough to make basic conversation with most villagers, unless the accent is extremely heavy, or the conversation goes too fast. Despite being shy by nature, I have forced myself to speak, no matter how ridiculous I sound. Italians are encouraging and forgiving, which makes it much easier.

Still, I have made some epic mistakes. A few years ago, I tried using the word for brother-in-law, *cognato,* when making family introductions to some Italian friends. Instead, I mistakenly used the word *coniglio.* I pointed to my sister's husband and announced: "This is Earl, my rabbit."

Another example is how Jess and I both pronounced "*Il conto, per favore,*" which means "The check, please." This is an important phrase to know, since Italians will let you sit at a table for as long as you like until you ask for the check. For years, we mispronounced *conto* as *canto,* which means we were saying, "The song, please." Which now explains why a couple of good-natured waiters broke out into song upon our request. Jess once even asked for *il gatto,* which is a cat. Some days things come out all wrong in English, much less another language.

Italians tend to be direct, with little beating about the bush. This might be nothing new for a New Yorker, but for a Southerner, it can seem a little abrupt at times. If something is beautiful, they say it is beautiful: *Che*

bello! If something is ugly, they call it like it is: *Che brutto.* I once asked an Italian friend if he liked the restoration job on our front door. "It's okay," he responded, with facial expressions and hand gestures, communicating "It's not bad, but it could have been better." I've really grown to appreciate this directness and have learned if you don't want the honest answer, you shouldn't ask the question.

Besides connection with the local villagers, there is also a community of expatriates who speak English and spend varying amounts of time in the area, from full time to a few months out of the year like us. Meeting other expats from other countries and all parts of the United States provides another form of connection with people we would normally never meet on Knob Lick Road in Kentucky.

Expats share a common love for their adopted country and the shared experience of discovering a culture through full immersion. We come from a variety of political, geographical, and faith backgrounds, yet we have an innate connection. We can instantly bond over recommendations for favorite restaurants, local events, craftspeople, and specialty shops, or give and ask advice about everything from home renovations to regional customs. We come to know and like each other as we share conversation over aperitivo and dinner. This is one of the greatest things about travel: We learn to love people outside of policies and politics.

For all the wonderful parts of meeting other foreigners, we all still come to Italy and love Italy for the Italians. While an English-speaking social circle may be the most comfortable, we push ourselves beyond, stretch into the uncomfortable, risk sounding and looking absurd, and try to bridge the language gap bit by bit. We are intentional about spending time with our Italian friends while speaking only Italian, a way to grow our language skills and grow the connection between us.

⁎⁎⁎

Years ago, when we drove in Italy before GPS and spoke almost no Italian, we learned there is an aggressive form of sign language used while driving, but it was only in recent years that I realized there is a language within the Italian language based solely on hand gestures. An entire language learned from childhood, with motions for everything from being hungry, to something going on and on, to a comment on how someone is sharp in an opportunistic way. There are around a dozen gestures related to food alone.

Recently, I passed a *nonna* (grandmother) on the street pushing a child in a stroller. The child was under a year old, not talking yet, but when he saw me, he pressed his index finger into the side of his cheek, twisted it, and pointed up. In those simple gestures, he told me he was going to eat something good in an upstairs apartment.

Words are used, and often lots of them, in boisterous rapid-fire. We have often observed loud discussions between Italians accompanied by wild gesticulations and intense looks. When it seems the two parties are on the verge of fisticuffs, there's a smile, a shrug, and a pleasant *ciao* as they go on their way.

Another nonverbal habit is "The Stare." This is a full-on stare for several uncomfortable seconds, sometimes open-mouthed and sometimes not, directed at you by a stranger, despite how much you might smile. A year ago, one of my country cousins visited us for a week. She's had a hard life and more than a few tussles in her early years. One day, we were walking in a neighboring village when she sidled next to me and whispered through a clenched jaw, "Why is that man staring at me?"

"It's nothing. A normal reaction to someone unknown, just curiosity." I patted her arm as she cast one last uncertain look back at the offender. A stare can be an invitation to fight where we come from, yet this stare is innocent curiosity and dissipates once an introduction is made. Even in our modern society where many formalities are lost, we still value the art of the introduction.

Sometimes superstitions impact connections in Italy, and for an unaware foreigner, it can be mystifying. Once, when Jess and I were introduced to several Italians by a mutual friend, we both reached out to shake hands and then reached across to shake the other hands. The Italians recoiled as if a rattlesnake had appeared in our midst, so we were left reaching into space with no hands to grab. They laughed and then shuffled around so no arms would cross during the handshaking.

Our friend explained it was considered bad luck to cross arms while shaking hands. We noticed this same thing happens when a toast is raised, and glasses are clinked. You never cross other clinking glasses. Instead, you hold back and wait, and then you reach for whomever you missed. While I'm not

superstitious, I have somehow adopted this custom and find myself holding back when people cross arms to clink glasses at home.

Business connections have their own little rules and customs, a few of which I have learned in the process of renovating our house in Italy. First, there must be an initial face-to-face meeting. Italians are very uncomfortable doing business over email, phone, or text, unless there has been an initial in-person meeting. Even when engaging someone to do small jobs like landscaping, pruning our few trees, or cleaning the cistern, an initial meeting is required.

I have also learned not to rush the conversation toward the financial arrangement. Italians want time to meet in person and grasp the scope of the project, and in a small village, there is also the expectation of some exchange of personal information. The financial arrangement is the last point to be discussed, and often it is done with a wrinkling of the nose, a turning away of the face, as if smelling something unpleasant.

When the job is complete, then there is a second meeting before payment, to make sure the job has been done properly. Tuscans seem to feel a strong desire for their work, what they have created, to be fully pleasing. Only after both parties are happy with the work is payment made. It is the very last thing to be done, as if to stretch out the relationship as long as possible before the conclusion.

✦

While our village is tiny, and it's easy to soon know at least most of the faces, if not names, it's also surprising to me how often I run into people I know in villages forty-five minutes to an hour away, making southern Tuscany feel quite small.

My British neighbors told me about an experience they recently had when they went to a neighboring town for dinner at a restaurant. They sat down, placed their food order, and then chose the wine. The waiter suddenly got a strange look on his face. *Did we order something wrong? A bad choice?* they wondered with no time to ask. He was off to the kitchen, and they were left in confusion about his reaction.

A few minutes later, a group of four entered the restaurant and were seated at the table next to them. Our friends recognized the new arrivals as

the producer of the wine they had just ordered, and then it made sense. The waiter must have known the winemaker of the bottle they selected would be seated next to them very shortly, hence the strange expression as he tried to puzzle out the coincidence.

Someone asked me the other day what drew us to Italy. I began listing the many factors, the art, history, architecture, landscape, craftsmanship, food, wine, and then I paused and realized while all those things are incredible attributes of a beautiful country, those qualities were only amenities to the people in our village and the connections we made.

Bring Italy Home

❖ When traveling to another culture, learn a few words and expressions in the language, like "please," "thank you," and some other basic phrases.

❖ If you regularly encounter someone from another culture in your town, make a connection by learning some words in their native language.

❖ Consider reading *The Divine Comedy* by Dante Alighieri, an Italian narrative poem in three parts.

❖ Watch the movie *A Roman Holiday*.

Panzanella

INGREDIENTS

5 cups stale bread
1 lb. Roma tomatoes, chopped and
   drained
1¼ cups peeled and diced cucumber
1 cup fresh basil

½ cup extra-virgin olive oil
2 T. red wine vinegar
1 tsp. sea salt
½ tsp. black pepper
Basil leaves for garnish

DIRECTIONS

Put the stale bread in a medium bowl, add water to cover it, then stir until the bread
is separated. Drain the excess water and then place the bread in a large bowl.

   Toss the bread with the remaining ingredients, mix well, and serve cold. Garnish
with basil leaves.

YIELD: 4 to 6 servings

5

Vi Aspettiamo

{WE WAIT FOR YOU}

Hospitality is not, "How can I make myself look good?"
but "How can I make others feel loved?"
—CASSIE PATTILLO

Contribute to the needs of the saints and seek to show hospitality.
—THE APOSTLE PAUL, LETTER TO THE ROMANS

I hung up the phone and frowned. I had just called to make a dinner reservation for the next week and the response was "*Vi aspettiamo.* We wait for you." In my effort to speak in Italian, did I mistakenly say we were coming now?

I imagined my friends at the restaurant standing at the door, glancing at the clock, waiting for me to make an appearance even though my visit was days away. It was silly, of course. They were taking orders, pouring drinks, and plating exquisite food. But somehow by saying, "We wait for you," they made me feel a little extra special.

I have now learned Tuscans often use the words *vi aspettiamo* when a dinner reservation is made or after an invitation has been extended. Literally translated, it means "we wait for you." This simple phrase offers the core of Tuscan hospitality in the implied expectation of a visitor's arrival. It's more than just saying, "We are looking forward to your visit." It's an anticipation, a preparation, and an invitation.

We received a dinner invitation from Italian friends for an evening in their home. It was pizza night in the village, the day the alimentari makes pizza for anyone who orders by lunchtime, so I figured pizza would be the evening fare.

We arrived at their garden gate to see a beautiful table covered in a cloth and set with six place settings. Next to it was a smaller table for drinks. In one glance, we immediately realized this was something special. Pizza would have been fine—but seeing the amount of preparation made us feel anticipated and honored.

<hr />

The idea of being anticipated carries over into overnight stays. I like it when a hotel knows we are arriving—unlike my non-planning husband who often wants to see what last-minute deals or upgrades we might be given when reservations have not been made. I will admit we have enjoyed some lovely rooms without reservations, but there is something nice about the way you are received when you have been anticipated. A bedside light is on, or perhaps you're greeted by a handwritten card of welcome, or even a basket of fruit or a vase of flowers. All these details go into making a guest feel wanted.

For many years, our home was the place where business and ministry partners landed when they visited our town. Later, we renovated an old house on a prominent corner to serve as a company guesthouse. We added another, and then decided to add three more and go public with our little hospitality venture. We currently have twenty-two rooms, two restaurants and a catering group, a gift shop, and a spa.

I've tried to apply this Italian concept of *vi aspettiamo* for our home and inn guests by thinking through all the details of what they might need and desire while they stay with us. Will our guests need to wash or iron clothes? Will they need a fan or a sleep machine at night? What kind of coffee do they prefer? What books might they like to have nearby if they have trouble

falling asleep? A soft blanket and a comfortable chair for late-night or early-morning reading?

Serving sparkling water to dinner guests is a detail I've brought back with me to Kentucky from Italy. The most iconic and storied sparkling water is San Pellegrino, presented in elegant green glass bottles and exported from Italy all over the world. A friend once told me offering San Pellegrino water at dinners made her feel so special—it communicates how happy we are to have guests by bringing out the best water, as if tap is not good enough for company. A figurative killing of the fatted calf.

Whether guests are arriving or not, cut flowers are usually scattered around our house in various shapes and sizes of small glass containers. In the summer, I grow my own zinnias or cockscombs for this purpose, and I often gather snippets of oregano, mint, or rosemary for the greenery.

Cockscombs are a particular favorite because they can be dried and used throughout the winter. In summer, the cockscombs grow as tall as me, with heads of soft velvety blooms, making them appear like stick people standing in my rock garden. Cockscombs are curious old-fashioned plants, named for their resemblance to a rooster comb, but despite their almost comedic look, they connect me to my mother, who is now several years gone. She loved all plants and flowers, but especially ruby-red cockscombs, partly because her mother used to grow them in her country garden. On drives through the Tuscan countryside, I often see these flowers, and for a moment, I feel as if I can almost hear a whisper of presence from my mother and grandmother.

For winter, in addition to the dried cockscombs, I might buy a bouquet from the grocery store and make it last by removing the flowers as they fade and rearranging the remaining ones. If I can't make it to the grocery, I snip some green from the holly, pine, or boxwoods to bring a little life inside during the winter months.

Sometimes I place one big arrangement on the dinner table, moved away when everyone is seated, or several small arrangements mixed with votive candles. I avoid forcing guests to crane their necks around a large arrangement to see the person on the other side. These small candles are inexpensive, versatile, and easy to position in various places in the room. They add to a festive mood, and don't have headache-triggering heavy scents.

While bright lights are needed for a working environment, when it is time to enjoy a meal, the lighting is lowered to signal relaxation and communion together. In addition to candles, dimmer switches, soft music, and a fire in cool weather can set the stage for a lovely evening. Finally, the porch light is illuminated for a last symbol of welcome and promise for nurturing hospitality.

While the anticipation is part of the joy, sometimes unexpected encounters can be just as delightful. Right after we purchased a house in the village, we transitioned from being regular tourists to people who were now a part of the community: adopted *montanini*.

Many times, as we paused to talk to locals on the street, we were invited into their homes for a tour of their living spaces and gardens. We were always offered something to drink—*caffè*, espresso, prosecco, or an *aperitivo analcolico* (a nonalcoholic drink made with bitter citrus). Back then we struggled to communicate, but somehow it didn't matter while we toured their homes, commented on photographs, and enjoyed the flowers in their gardens.

This reminded me so much of my upbringing where unexpected visitors were a part of our life. In the country and in small towns, people will simply "stop by." Maybe they're passing by your home and just have a last-minute urge to pull in and say hello. Or perhaps they come to your house with the intention of a visit, taking a chance you might be home.

There was an unspoken rule in my house: Anyone who entered must be offered a drink. This was mostly sweet iced tea, or perhaps a soda or water or coffee, depending on the time of day. In the homes of my aunts, I always knew a freshly brewed pitcher of iced tea would be in their refrigerators, and a glass would be offered.

⁓⁓✦⁓⁓

Years ago, early in our marriage, Jess and I were driving around in the Kentucky countryside and admiring old Federal houses. Jess knew of a couple who lived in an important old house in a very old area of the county called Preachersville. He wanted me to see the outside of the house, so we pulled into the driveway for a quick look. Laura, one of the owners, was coming from the barn in her muck boots. We waved and she walked over to chat.

We apologized for disturbing her and said we only wanted to see the outside of the house. Not put off by our protestations, she ushered us inside for an impromptu tour. Laura pulled cheese and wine from her refrigerator and crackers from her cupboard. She taught me it's possible to always anticipate guests, even when you don't know who they are or when they will stop. With cheese and crackers on hand and a little something to drink, we're always ready for last-minute visits.

Anticipation and expectation can be provided in small ways. While grand gestures are lovely, it can be kept simple, personal, and intentional.

Bring Italy Home

- ❖ Use votive candles, cut flowers, and sparkling water to give guests a feeling of being anticipated.

- ❖ Keep cheese and crackers on hand, along with a bottle of prosecco or sparkling water, or even sparkling apple cider.

- ❖ Read *The Tuscan Child* by Rhys Bowen.

- ❖ Watch the Oscar-winning *Life Is Beautiful*.

Cream Cheese and Hot Pepper Jelly

In addition to cheese and crackers, this is one of my favorite standbys for unexpected guests. Both are easy to keep for months at a time and make a delicious sweet-and-salty, spicy-and-creamy snack.

INGREDIENTS

1 (8 oz.) block cream cheese, softened to room temperature

Hot pepper jelly, red or green

Hard crackers, seasoned only with salt

DIRECTIONS

Remove the cream cheese from its package and place it on the center of a serving plate. With a table knife, smooth down the rough edges. Pour the hot pepper jelly over the top of the block of cream cheese so it drips down the sides. Add a small serving knife, then place the crackers around the outside of the dish or in a separate dish. Best when the cream cheese has an hour or so to soften at room temperature.

For the Italian version of this, substitute ricotta for the cream cheese and use small bites of freshly baked bread instead of crackers.

YIELD: 10 to 12 servings

Aperitivo
{THE PREDINNER DRINK}

*Day offers two equally necessary sacraments—the benediction
of morning and the absolution of dusk. In the morning coffee
blesses and in the evening wine absolves.*

—MICHAEL FOLEY

Aperitivo has Latin roots meaning "to open," and is literally the
opening of the evening, meant to prepare the appetite for dinner.
In Italy, a place where food and wine are served together, this also means
some snacks or light bites. It is a time to stop and rest, to transition from the
day's work, to unwind, to relax into the evening and prepare for the dinner
to follow.

I remember an early aperitivo experience on our first stay in the village as
I was writing my second novel. We noticed an elegant woman coming and
going from a mysterious wooden door, and we suspected this door might
lead to some beautiful gardens we saw below our apartment. One day, Jess
saw her on the street and introduced himself, and fortunately, she spoke

English. Jess asked her about the gardens below and she extended an invitation to view them two days hence.

We arrived at Benedetta's door in late afternoon at the appointed time. We were ushered graciously into her home, shown around, then taken outside to a terrace overlooking a beautiful Italian garden. Benedetta shared the history of the garden and showed us its different parts, from formal to less formal, even the place where the laundry had been done in centuries past, now taken over by sleeping bats.

After the tour, she had us sit on the terrace and enjoy the view while she brought out a tray with potato chips, *grissini* (thin and crunchy breadsticks), cheese, and olives, along with a bottle of chilled prosecco. We thought our visit would end when the tour was over, but this was a cue for us to stay a bit longer. It was a simple presentation, but a perfect way to extend the visit for another hour. We each shared some of our story and established the beginning of a friendship.

While the new relationship was the main jewel of the visit, I also appreciated my first aperitivo experience and how it makes entertaining so easy and light. Not too much preparation, not too long of a visit, but just enough to make a connection.

In our village, an aperitivo will begin around six or six thirty in the evening and last until around seven thirty or eight at the latest, which often collides with dusk, so the last of the day is savored and bade farewell. Dinner will be had elsewhere; this is a shorter time to visit over something to drink, maybe prosecco, an Aperol spritz, or a light white wine and some nibbles.

With many aperitivi experiences now, I can say the food offerings range from potato chips to cheese, crackers, salami, and bruschetta. The burden of preparation is light, and the potential for conversation and friendship is rich.

For a slightly longer evening without all the preparations of a proper dinner, the *apericena* is a more modern concept bridging the aperitivo and dinner. *Cena* means "dinner" in Italian, so the apericena is what we might call "heavy appetizers" with a few more finger food choices. This simple gathering requires a bit more preparation than an aperitivo and indicates a longer experience, but still without all the fuss of a multicourse dinner.

Sometimes I will add a soup and dessert to the end of an apericena for a heartier ending.

A note about wine pours: An Italian wine pour stops at the curve of the wine glass, much smaller than what we see in the United States. Wine glasses may be large, but partly to allow the wine to fully breathe outside the bottle, not for the purpose of filling up. Sparkling and still water are always welcome in addition to wine. The point is to enjoy the conversation, the food, and the wine, with all three in harmony and balance, as you open the evening and end the day.

Bring Italy Home

✤ Host an aperitivo for friends and neighbors. Set the expectations on food and drink and the time frame and have fun. Keep it simple and remember it's all about connection for a short while.

✤ Have your friends over for a spritzer night. Provide the ingredients for various spritzers, nonalcoholic and alcoholic, and let everyone have fun creating their own from an ingredient bar.

Aperitivo Menu Ideas

Bruschetta or crostini
Caprese skewers
Olives
Pecorino cheese: fresh, semi-aged,
   or aged—or all three (sliced, or set
   out in wedges with a cheese knife)
Salami and prosciutto (tip: fold the
   meats so they're not just lying flat
   on the plate—they're easier to pick
   up with a fork and look nicer)

Aperol spritz
Nonalcoholic fruit spritzer
Prosecco
Sparkling and still water
White or red wine

Crostini means "little toasts." These goodies are made by thinly slicing bread and toasting, grilling, or even frying it so it becomes crispy. A brushing of olive oil and a sprinkling of sea salt make them delightful snacks on their own to serve with soup, or as a background for other toppings. If you don't want to make your own, a brand I really like is Bruschettini, the Classico Virgin Olive Oil version, made by Asturi and available in most party stores.

Aperol Spritz

INGREDIENTS

1 large orange slice, halved
Prosecco

Aperol
Tonic water or club soda

DIRECTIONS

Place one half of the orange slice in the bottom of a large wine glass. Fill with ice.

Add equal parts of prosecco, Aperol, and either tonic water or club soda, depending on whether you want to emphasize the bitter (by adding the tonic water) or the sweet (by adding the more neutral club soda). Stir gently and garnish with the other half of the orange slice.

Nonalcoholic Fruit Spritzers

INGREDIENTS

Sparkling water or club soda
Fruit juice

Simple syrup
Fruit for garnish

DIRECTIONS

In a glass, pour one part sparkling water, one part fruit juice, and then add simple syrup to taste, depending on the sweetness of the juice you choose. Add a slice of fruit or a berry and stir. With so many fun combinations to try—depending on the fruit in season and preferences for sweet, tart, and bitter—limes, strawberries, grapes, cranberries, raspberries, blueberries, and oranges are some possibilities. Have fun creating your own spritzer.

7

La Tavola

{THE TABLE}

A tavola non si invecchia. At the table [with good friends and family] you do not become old.

—ITALIAN PROVERB

While *la tavola* translates to "the table," the meaning is nuanced far beyond a piece of flat wood holding food and cutlery. It is about friends and family interacting together over food, making connections and conversation, while both body and soul are nurtured. To receive an invitation to sit at someone's table is an honor. In fact, there is an Italian proverb: "*Non abbiamo mai mangiato insieme,*" which means "We have never eaten together." This is a way of saying, "We are not close," and slightly implies a dislike or distrust of someone.

My mother never hosted people for dinner outside of an annual family cookout or Christmas potluck, so I never experienced a dinner party modeled in any way. In fact, in most of my early years, any invites were to cookouts, soup suppers, church potlucks, picnics, and pizza.

As a working single adult, I experienced the world of banquet and fine dining through my job, but the mysteries of setting a table eluded me. There was never a reason. My own hosting as a young adult followed the pattern laid out by my mother and my friends whereby a pot of chili or delivered pizza served as the entrée and was taken buffet-style.

When Jess wanted to host our first dinner party as a newly married couple, the idea overwhelmed me. Where to start? I brought out the good china and silverware, placed each item on the table according to the diagram in the etiquette book, folded cloth napkins, then dashed around the farm looking for wildflowers to arrange for the table. In the kitchen, I prepared a meat dish, veggies, salad, and dessert from scratch in one messy, chaotic cook-fest. With a last wild scramble to clean the kitchen, clean myself, and prepare the drinks, I hoped our guests would be late.

Honestly, I could hardly wait for the evening to be over. Forget the meal and the people—I was ready to curl up with a bowl of popcorn and a Doris Day movie. It was not a pleasant experience for me, and I'm sure the guests sensed my exhaustion as well.

A moment of inspiration hit at a friend's house one night. After shedding my coat, I offered the obligatory, "Can I do anything to help?"

"Sure, grab a knife and cut the carrots." She offered me a drink and we laughed and talked while I helped prepare the salad. I noticed how calm and relaxed she was, as if the food wasn't as important as the time we were spending together. She wanted to visit with me, to find out what was going on in my life and how I was feeling about certain events. We had a wonderful evening, and it changed my whole attitude about having people over for dinner.

People are more important than the meal, the house, or the presentation. My friend understood hospitality, while I was trying to learn to entertain and wearing myself out in the process. I thought all my work was for the guest, but it was really all about me, and how I wanted to appear confident in my new role.

Nowadays, I have a routine that makes hosting much easier. But even if something goes wrong, I've learned guests don't mind at all, and often these mishaps make for a memorable evening. Multiple times, I've broken or spilled something just before guests arrive, only to have them pitch in and help with the cleanup. No one cares, honestly. If you don't mind, they won't mind. On the other hand, I once attended a dinner party where the host was

aggravated over a mistake by the caterer early in the evening. He fumed and sulked all night and it ruined the party for him, the caterer, and his guests. If he had not minded, neither would we.

Nowadays, when guests arrive, we sit and chat for forty-five minutes to an hour, with light bites and beverages, before sitting down to dinner. I enjoy the company and am not in a hurry to rush them out the door. Meals may be nothing fancier than soup and salad or some of our homegrown vegetables from the garden, and I've learned the practice of preparing things in advance and not selecting menu items requiring last-minute preparations.

Not long ago, we went to dinner at the home of some friends in the village. They live in a tower, full of ancient character but somewhat limiting in the ability to host a very large group. Their extended table for eight took up most of the room. Several jams and jellies, both sweet and spicy, were placed in the center with a bowl of fresh ricotta and a basket of fresh sliced bread. We took the bread, spread a bit of ricotta on it, then added some of the jams as we talked and laughed.

Next, they served a delicious *ribollita*, eaten with a fork instead of a spoon, and maybe the best I have ever tasted. Chicken and vegetables followed, with ice cream for dessert. It made for one of the most memorable evenings for us—to be welcomed into someone's home, to work on our Italian through lively conversation, and to share food prepared by their own hands, assembled and arranged ahead of time so that when we arrived, they were relaxed and not distracted, which in turn relaxed us.

The first time I realized how often I use buffet to serve food was during the visit of an Italian teenager, Matteo, the son of our friends. One day, he asked, "Why is food laid out on a counter and not served at the table?" Why indeed? It's convenient, for one thing. All the food in one place avoids having to ask for this or that. I don't have to carry everything to the dining room and back when the meal is over. People can take what they want. I tried to explain all our reasons, but he was not sold.

After experiencing Italian dinners, I realized buffet-style puts the focus on the food, not interaction, as the main event. In fact, conversation is stilted because people arrive at the table in dribbles, pop up and down to fetch something they missed, or go for a second serving. With everyone seated at a table, more eye contact and interaction naturally happen as food is passed back and forth.

Matteo's question made me think about why we do what we do. If everyone can squeeze together at one table, why not try it? With thirteen family members around the Thanksgiving table last year, I explained the new family-style plan to my family and why we were doing it. Laughter and jokes followed, with a great deal of exaggerated eye contact as dishes were passed, but we had far more conversation and laughter than our previous dinners. It's our new tradition.

Bring Italy Home

- ❖ Try family-style dining next time you are tempted to do buffet.

- ❖ Create dinner parties with minimal last-minute preparations, and when there are some, involve your guests.

- ❖ Read *The Leopard* by Giuseppe Tomasi di Lampedusa, an Italian classic.

- ❖ Watch *Tea with Mussolini*.

- ❖ Listen to some old recordings of the famous Enrico Caruso.

Aglione Sauce

Traditional *aglione* sauce in our area of Tuscany is made from the big garlic raised in the Val di Chiana, a type of elephant garlic, and is often served with *pici* pasta, and called *pici all'aglione*. Any pasta works with this simple sauce, and if you can't locate elephant garlic, normal is fine.

INGREDIENTS

¼ cup extra-virgin olive oil

4 to 5 garlic cloves

2 cups canned, peeled Roma tomatoes

½ tsp. of sugar

⅛ tsp. of chili pepper flakes (depending on taste)

½ tsp. of salt

1 pound pici pasta, cooked (or spaghetti if you don't have pici; time the cooking so the pasta is ready at the same time as the sauce)

Grated pecorino cheese

DIRECTIONS

Drizzle the olive oil in a pan or pot over medium heat and add the garlic. After the garlic sizzles and turns to golden brown, turn the pan to low heat and add the tomatoes. Add sugar, chili flakes, and salt to taste. Simmer for 15 to 20 minutes. Toss your favorite cooked pasta into the sauce and serve. Sprinkle the top with grated pecorino cheese.

YIELD: 6 servings

8

Il Cibo

{THE FOOD}

Prima si mangia e poi si ragiona. First we eat and then we think.
—ITALIAN PROVERB

There may be no subject more impassioned, debated, and discussed in Italy than food. It is a reason for gathering, a sign of friendship, a source of pride, and a strong connection to the land, history, and culture. No matter the topic of conversation among my Tuscan friends, whether it be business or social, the subject always turns to food.

Tuscan food is based on using simple, fresh ingredients with an emphasis on what is in season. Every time I sit down with an Italian friend to write down a recipe, I know there will likely be no exact measurements. Cooking is often done by feeling and sensing the right amount—after years and years of practice—an impossible nuance to impart in a recipe. While the precise ingredients may be a little loose, each cook says with the solemnity of a monk, "The ingredients must be fresh, and the quality must be good."

❦

Cucina povera (poor kitchen) is an expression often used to describe the roots of the Tuscan diet, based on the peasant lifestyle, with ingredients sourced locally and inexpensively. Flavorful herbs, garlic, mushrooms, truffles, game from the forest, *pici* and *tagliatelle* pasta, and pecorino cheese, along with white beans, chicory greens, and chopped tomato, form the basic ingredients for many Tuscan dishes, with accessibility to good meat from the Chianina beef and the Cinta Senese pork as a more recent addition.

Tuscan bread is made without salt and works perfectly as a conduit for food. This practice may come from an ancient tax on salt, or possibly it's because the bread then has a longer shelf life (even if stale) since the salt draws moisture and hence mold—or maybe it's simply a contrast to the salty meats and cheeses. Most Tuscans will clean their plate with a piece of bread to sop up any remaining sauce, and this act even has a name: *fare la scarpetta*, or to make the "little shoe." Just as a shoe might drag up what's on the ground, so the bread can drag up the last bit of sauce. In a culture where most families lived in poverty, to leave food on the plate bordered on sin.

Pici pasta, a rustic thick spaghetti derived from the Val di Chiana, is an example of classic Tuscan peasant food. It is on every local menu in our area and is often made in-house. As with most recipes from the region, the ingredients are simple: only flour, water, and egg, with the egg a more recent addition.

⁓ ❧ ⁓

After our local historian and his wife invited us to dinner in their home, I asked him for a couple of the recipes. I expected him to text the ingredients and instructions back to me. Instead, my doorbell rang—he had come in person to explain the process, as this subject was far too important for a text and must be properly understood. As I took notes, Andrea went through in detail how he made the hot pepper marmalade used with ricotta as a topping for bread, reminiscent of our cream cheese and hot pepper jelly pairing.

We then went on to his recipe for ribollita, a stew made with beans, stale bread, greens, and herbs. He began to explain, then stopped and said, "Next time, you come to our house, and I will show you. It's better to see it."

In Italy, there are even some recipes too important to explain. They must be demonstrated and experienced. This may explain the number of cooking schools in the country: There are two in our tiny village of four hundred people. Visitors arrive on a Sunday, then cook, eat, drink, and tour for a week before going home the following Saturday.

While Italians might shrug their shoulders and say "*È la vita*. It's life" about somewhat serious issues, my experience is the opposite when the subject is food. Everyone has an opinion and a preferred way to do it. A village friend once told me about a community group where the agenda was delayed for thirty minutes while they could discuss the best time and way to slice cheese for an upcoming event. I have observed myself how any kind of gathering over various topics often ends up with some form of food discussion.

Marco, the local tree pruner, came once in the fall to deliver some porcini mushrooms found in the forest. I asked him for a recommendation on how to prepare them. He explained how I should cut off the *non buoni* (not-so-nice) piece at the bottom, clean them gently, slice them, dip them in egg and flour and salt, then fry them in a pan. This explanation was finished by kissing his five fingers and then releasing them into the air with a flourish.

It's not abnormal to be shown photos of mushrooms or truffles on an Italian's phone as if they are showing off their grandchildren, and there is always advice on how things should be properly prepared.

When the cachi tree in our garden ripened one autumn with persimmon-like fruit, we took some to our neighbors. They told us to add some apples to our bowl of fruit to hasten the ripening. In a few days, they would be perfect. This was followed by a hand gesture indicating the level of perfection. Sure enough, in a few days the fruit was at the peak of ripeness. I have no idea if there is any science to the apples or not, but it's far more romantic to think the apples were helping the persimmons along in fruity camaraderie.

When the subject of chicken came up recently, one of my Italian friends scowled and shook his head as he recounted seeing a foreigner order chicken on their pizza. "*No, mai!* Never! *Il pollo è un secondo, non per la pizza.* Chicken is a main dish, not for pizza." You won't find chicken on salads around here either. Chicken has its place as the star of the show, not a supporting role. Tuna, however, is allowed to grace a salad.

Seasonal offerings are showcased on the local menus, such as the two or three weeks in the spring when the garlic flower blooms and complements pasta. Or when the spring greens and radishes are in season, creating flavorful salads, or the summer freshness of basil and tomatoes combine to make the most delicious bruschetta. I recently had a strawberry dessert with basil, two flavors I've never combined, but with both in season and at the peak of freshness, it was exquisite.

In autumn, mushrooms, truffles, and chestnuts take the stage, and in winter, the focus is on root vegetables, beans, meat, pastas, and the comforting ribollita soup. As an old Italian proverb says, "*Ogni frutto ha la sua stagione. Every fruit has its season.*"

Each food has its role, there is an order to the meal, and things are best eaten in season. Even with this, there are strong opinions within regions of Italy on how food is made, each region confident their own is the best way. My Italian tutor is *Napoletano* (from Naples) but has lived in Tuscany for many years. We often discuss food as part of our Italian lessons, naturally, and if we are talking about a dish common to both Tuscany and Naples, he always says the dish from Naples is better and the way his mother prepared it is the best.

Another southerner from Puglia is working on a renovation down the street in our village. We visited the site recently, only to spend ten minutes with him discussing the food from the heel of the boot, specifically the *orecchiette* (ear-shaped) pasta. His face lit up and he explained how his mother makes it, the sauce she prepares to go with it, and then used multiple hand gestures to emphasize how delicious it is. By the end of the conversation, I was ready to hop in the car and drive south in the hope of sitting at his *mamma's* table.

Sometimes before we leave Italy in the fall and go into the long nights of winter and the many months before our return, I try to consume Tuscany by eating my favorite pastas, sipping my favorite wines, eating the crostini and bruschetta, and indulging in a last cornetto con crema. It's impossible, of course. I will arrive home and be hungry for Italy in a matter of days, but I have practiced taking a bit of Italy home, like newly harvested oil from our friend Enzo, along with spices, and pasta from the market. It is a reminder and a promise, connecting me to this place I love.

Bring Italy Home

❖ Try your hand at making homemade pasta. Prepare for dinner the same evening or store in the refrigerator a day ahead.

❖ Adjust recipes to focus on simple ingredients rather than leaning on heavy sauces.

❖ Source good-quality olive oil and vinegar for your salads.

❖ Watch *Stanley Tucci: Searching for Italy*, a series about regional dishes.

A note on olive oil: Extra-virgin olive oil (EVOO) is necessary for any Italian recipe, and there are many bad options on supermarket shelves. What is extra-virgin olive oil, and how do you know which is the real thing?

Olive oil is made when the olives are pressed to extract the oil. There are several food grades of olive oil, but the least processed, healthiest, and best for flavor is the first pressing, called extra-virgin olive oil. Check for a harvest date on the back of the bottle. If there is no harvest date, don't purchase it. If there is a harvest date, then check to make sure the oil was harvested within the last year. The date will show up as 2024/2025 to indicate oil harvest in the fall of the 2024 season. Most experts agree it is best to consume oil within eighteen months of harvest.

Carolina's Pici Pasta

Carolina makes delicious pici pasta based on her grandmother's recipe. This rustic pasta is like a thick spaghetti and provides a filling dish. Italian "00" flour is a very refined flour, while "0" flour is less refined, most like all-purpose flour.

INGREDIENTS

2½ cups Italian "00" flour
1½ cups + 3 T. "0" flour
1 egg

Pinch of salt
2 cups tepid water
Extra-virgin olive oil

DIRECTIONS

Put both flours together in a bowl. Mix gently with your hands.

Pour the flour on a clean work surface and make a little well in the middle.

Add the egg and salt to the well and mix, using a fork.

Begin adding the water, a little at a time, to the middle of the flour and mix, using your hands.

Keep working with the water and your hands until the dough comes together. You can then start kneading the dough until the dough is the right consistency (you will see and feel this).

Roll the dough into a circle (keep it quite thick). Add a drizzle of olive oil to the top and massage it in gently to cover the entirety of the top with oil. Then cover the dough with either baking paper or plastic film, leaving it to rest for at least 30 minutes (if you are in a very warm environment, you might consider putting the dough in the fridge to rest). This can also be a time to make a sauce for the pasta.

When the dough has rested, slice off a little piece and start rolling into a worm-like shape using the palms of your hands. Roll and stretch each small piece of the dough to form long worm shapes (the pasta should look like long, thick spaghetti).

Pici is ready to cook immediately. Bring a pot of salted water to boil, add a bit of olive oil to keep the pasta from sticking, and add the pici pasta. Cook until *al dente* (slightly chewy), approximately 9 minutes.

YIELD: 6 servings

La Digestione
{THE DIGESTION}

Chi mangia piano vive sano. Those who eat slowly live healthy.
—ITALIAN PROVERB

If you are fortunate enough to go beyond being a tourist and dive a bit deeper into local Italian culture, you will soon discover within the all-important subject of food lies another important topic for Italians: the digestion.

There are certain digestive mantras, or even rules, abided by Italians all over the country. I visited Italy for years before I realized I was breaking a cardinal digestive rule by having an afternoon cappuccino. On a food tour in Rome, I learned how strongly Italians dislike the effects of milk after lunch.

Every aspect of the Italian food experience seems designed to make the most of our digestion, beginning with the bitters often used for aperitivo. The most well-known are Campari and Aperol, which give the diner a nice lower alcohol beginning to the meal. Bitters date back to ancient Roman nobles, who drank them for their restorative properties.

Mineral waters, drunk with each meal, are offered in both flat and *frizzante*, with the extra benefit of fizzy water settling the stomach. There are naturally carbonated springs, which is how sparkling mineral water originated as a drinking option, but many Tuscan households will add bicarbonate soda bought from the alimentari to create the bubbly.

Food is always taken with wine, which cuts the effects of the alcohol, and some think wine cuts the fat of the meal, making food and wine a fine partnership.

The meal is paced out with the antipasto, the *primo* (pasta course), *secondo* (meat course), and *contorni* (side dishes to go with the meat), and then the *dolce* (dessert), with each course offering time to digest before another is brought. Fast eaters are forced to sit and wait until the slowest eaters at the table finish with their course before another is brought. Coffee is always served after the dessert, not with it, and of course black. Finally, the meal is finished with a *digestivo*.

While grappa, *limoncello*, and others are known best in certain regions, the local digestive in our area is vin santo, best when paired with cantucci (crunchy almond biscotti).

Most of our friends make their own vin santo and even their own limoncello. Once, we enjoyed a lovely community lunch and many of the locals brought their own homemade *digestivi*, made from *mirto* (myrtle), which has roots in Sardinia, where many Tuscans emigrated from, bringing their sheepherding and cheese-making skills with them. Digestivi can be made from a variety of berries, fruits, roots, herbs, and nuts, and all boast purported medicinal qualities.

One day after exploring the Montalcino area, we were on our way home and had decided to take back roads through the Val d'Orcia, when a stunning structure rose up in the middle of the hills and gray landslides of the *crete senesi*, a rocky gray gravel feature giving the Val d'Orcia a near-moonscape appearance in parts. We pulled over and discovered this was Monte Oliveto, a Benedictine monastery. We toured the grounds, the gift shop, the sanctuary and cloister, their library, and then the pharmacy. The pharmacy was a large room at the end of a library, an ancient lab, with all sorts of bottles and contraptions for distilling herbs and botanicals to treat illnesses. Though it is only a museum today, it must have been an advanced place of healing years

ago by the looks of the size and scale of the containers and the shelves.

The Monte Oliveto monks still create a twenty-three-herb digestive based on a five-hundred-year-old recipe. The current steward and maker of the recipe is Brother Raffaele. The monk who runs the store at the abbey always tells me, "*Prendi solo un po*—take only a little," which is no problem since it tastes like medicine.

I have shared this digestivo with numerous friends who are convinced of the healing power. While the scientific evidence may be elusive, I can say with certainty most folks feel better after a sip of the monks' remedy.

❦

The digestive focus even extends to the use of spices. A few months ago, a house cleaner pulled most of the spices off my spice rack and wagged her finger at them—or me, I'm not sure which.

"*Da buttare via*. To throw away."

"Why?"

"*Male per la digestione*. Bad for digestion."

She showed me the expiration date and shot me an accusing look. The dates were expired by a year, even two years, she said, doing circular motions with her hand, palm up. They had to be thrown away.

It's difficult to imagine an American house cleaner examining a client's spice rack unless specifically asked to do so. Here in Italy, policing the digestion is second nature.

While the spices looked and smelled fine to me, under her penetrating gaze, I tossed them out. Thank goodness she wasn't cleaning my house in Kentucky. There's no telling what dangers lurk in the dark recesses of that spice cupboard.

Bring Italy Home

- Check your spice rack for long-expired spices. Focus on a select group of spices and make sure they are fresh.

- Be conscious of how fast you eat. Enjoy and savor each bite. Slow the pacing at family dinners.

- Read *Playing for Pizza* by John Grisham.

- Practice the order of wines and how to taste and pair.

A note about wines: An Italian wine tasting begins with the lightest wine, such as prosecco, progresses toward a rosato (rosé) and then a white wine, then moves to a variety of reds, ending with the fuller body red wines. It is done in this order so you can fully experience the more robust wines near the end of the tasting. Otherwise, you will not appreciate the lightness of a prosecco or rosato if you start with a heavy red. Similarly, when you pair food with wine, you want to consider how the wine will enhance the food and not overpower it.

Albo's Secret Agrumello Recipe

This is my favorite digestive, first tasted at 13 Gobbi, the village restaurant. The owner, Albo, speaks glowingly of the medicinal qualities, but I will leave that for you to decide.

INGREDIENTS

3 lemons
3 oranges
2 mandarins
1 pink grapefruit
1 liter alcohol, 96 percent

500 ml. (2 cups) water
700 g. (2½ cups) sugar
Juice of one orange
Juice of one lemon

DIRECTIONS

Wash the fruit very well. Peel the rinds. Be sure not to include the white pith, as it's too bitter.

Combine the rinds and alcohol in a glass jar, then seal the jar and leave it in a dark place for two weeks. After two weeks, boil the water and then mix in the sugar, the juice of an orange, and the juice of a lemon to produce the syrup. Let the syrup cool. Transfer the alcoholic infusion to the syrup by using a colander to separate the rinds. Bottle the mixture immediately and let it sit for two more weeks. Freeze the bottle and then savor your delicious *agrumello*!

10

La Casa

{THE HOUSE, THE HOME}

Simplicity is the ultimate sophistication.

—UNKNOWN

In Tuscany, when we first saw our future home, previously a nobleman's stable, it surprised and delighted us with so many features we longed for, as if it had been waiting for us to fly across the ocean and walk inside the front door. Even so, two weeks after closing, we realized we had just inadvertently embarked on an entire restoration project, despite it being the one thing we did not want to do.

My Kentucky farmhouse had gone through one renovation before I arrived on the scene and we have done several other house renovations over the years, but nothing of this magnitude. The many other renovations we tackled were for the purpose of guest lodgings or businesses. This was the first time I would live in a property I had restored for a few months out of the year.

Numerous decisions needed to be made in a short amount of time, all the while navigating a foreign language and foreign currency, converting metric measurements to feet and inches, and understanding how Italians live and what is normal for them.

There was a point early on when I had to make an overarching decision: Is this to be an American house in Tuscany or a Tuscan house occupied by Americans? We chose the latter, which guided all decisions.

There was never much of a question about building closets. Closets are a foreign concept, since every Tuscan home makes use of wardrobes, either stand-alone antiques or possibly modern systems assembled separately.

Living in a house without closets for clothing is a freeing experience. For one thing, my clothes are kept to a minimum here. There is a blanket chest I can use to store off-season clothes, but everything in season must hang in an antique wardrobe no bigger than a yard wide or be stored in my chest of drawers. Most people wear the same clothing items over and over in our little village. The sweater you see on someone three days in a week might be a high-quality piece of knitwear, but what a way to get your money's worth. There's no reason to wear a different outfit every day, if the clothing is clean.

***

Our bathrooms feature bidets, and while many Americans scratch their heads over this unfamiliar fixture, I have grown to appreciate them for the variety of purposes they can be used for—think little bathtub and the possibilities are endless.

Air-conditioning is very rare in Tuscan homes, especially the hilltop villages where breezes cool down the homes and the thick stone walls serve as excellent insulation. Our downstairs common area does not have air-conditioning—we simply open the doors and windows and let the air cool it down. Even in the heat of July and August, it is surprising how comfortable it is. We did compromise by installing a split unit in all the bedrooms. In hot weather, the unit is turned on before dinner and the bedroom door closed. By nighttime, the room is cool for sleeping, without the unit running all day.

Laundry normally doesn't have a room of its own and usually consists only of a washing machine and a drying rack. Often, the washer will be tucked into a kitchen or a bathroom. It's not common for Italians to have a home dryer unless they rent out rooms to foreign visitors. In a place with dry heat and low humidity, it makes sense. Coming from our humid Kentucky climate, I couldn't imagine not having a dryer, so I purchased one for our

Tuscan home despite conventional wisdom, but I'm not sure it was worth it. My clothes are still damp after they've spent two hours rolling around in the dryer, and I end up placing them on the drying rack anyway.

The Tuscan house has a bare minimum of storage space, which makes me think twice about every purchase I make. Will it have a place to reside? The answer is usually no, which is a natural curb to consumption.

Our life in Italy is nearly without a television altogether, but we do have a tiny one in the upstairs apartment only for the purpose of watching old-fashioned DVDs when weather pushes us inside. We often go weeks without watching any kind of film or shows. There's no need when there is so much to see outside on the terrace and so many people to visit with in the village.

After being invited into Italian homes, I noticed how many Italian couches are covered with a sheet. It had always been a mystery to me until I bought a white couch and went in search of a spray to protect from stains. After a great deal of hunting, I confirmed with an American friend such a spray doesn't exist in Italy, because as I later found out, Italy and the European Union are far stricter than the United States about harmful chemicals in products. The sheets are a way to protect the couches.

When we moved into our Tuscan home, another curious thing happened. Italian friends arrived for a visit bearing a heavy wool blanket as a gift. It resembled something the army might have issued during World War II. We pondered this mysterious gift and wondered exactly what we were supposed to do with it.

The Tuscan winters never get as cold as our Kentucky winters, but I soon learned their idea of cold and ours are very different. We often see the locals walking around in puffy coats when the temperature drops below seventy degrees. I later realized this heartfelt gift of a wool blanket was meant to keep us warm in the cold of winter when it dips below a shocking forty degrees.

Time after time, guests have declared they received the best night's sleep at our Tuscan house. While I have taken great care with selecting the right mattresses and pillows, I believe this deep sleep is partly due to the *sportelli* shutters, made of solid wood and created to close on the inside, completely shutting out the light and providing a cave-like setting for jetlagged and weary travelers.

Many homes in the village have *scuretti* or *persiane*, which are louvered shutters placed on the outside for the windows as well as for the doors. Sometimes, because of the heat, both outer and inner doors will be left open and then a fabric curtain—or even beads reminiscent of a 1970s disco—will hang as the divider between the house and the street, a quirky and fun feature.

I often return from Italy and realize how overly abundant my closets are in our Kentucky farmhouse and how easy it is to fill those closets. I am constantly policing my purchases in Italy. Is this necessary? Where will it be stored? How will it be used? I find most of our spending in Italy is on consumables and sharables: good food, fresh olive oil, a new vintage of wine.

All of this has made me rethink how I live on the other side of the water, and how I can live more like a Tuscan at home.

Bring Italy Home

❖ Limit clothing and shoes to a smaller area and keep them within a space budget.

❖ Dry your clothes outside on warm summer days.

❖ Read the book *Under the Tuscan Sun* by Frances Mayes. You may be familiar with the movie, but her poetic writing must be experienced.

❖ Watch *My House in Umbria*.

Carolina's Fried Sage Leaves

INGREDIENTS

¾ cup all-purpose flour
Pinch of salt
¾ cup beer or sparkling water

Peanut oil for frying
24 clean, large sage leaves

DIRECTIONS

Mix the flour and salt and then add the beer, little by little, blending with a fork or whisk until it is well mixed. Heat the peanut oil. You'll know the oil is ready when you flick droplets of water into the oil and it sizzles.

Dip the leaves one by one in the batter and drop in hot peanut oil. When golden brown, under 30 seconds, remove the leaves with a slotted spoon and lay them on a plate covered with paper towels to drain the excess oil. Sprinkle a bit of salt on top to taste. Serve hot.

YIELD: 12 servings

11

La Cucina

{THE KITCHEN}

La cucina piccola fa la casa grande. A small kitchen makes the house big.
—ITALIAN PROVERB

In late October, we were invited into a villager's home. In front of the window was a lovely planter with three healthy plants: rosemary, sage, and basil. I remarked on the vibrancy of the plants and my host responded, *"Ogni casa ha rosmarino, salvia, e basilico.* Every house has rosemary, sage, and basil." With these three most necessary ingredients, you can make an abundance of Italian dishes. With the addition of garlic, salt, pepper, lemon, and olive oil, you are prepared to make almost anything.

If we look at a house like a body, the kitchen must be the heart. Our Kentucky farmhouse kitchen is a large room big enough for a marble-top island and a table seating eight. It's the center of any activity or social function, where our friends and family linger over cups of coffee, meals, and conversation.

I've poked my head into many kitchens for both restaurants and homes and am always surprised at how Italian kitchens can sometimes be shockingly small and most are not air-conditioned, a challenge in the high heat of summer, yet the food produced by these kitchens is far superior to what I've tasted from much grander kitchens.

What I do find is an extremely functional space with the essential pasta pots, saucepans, rolling pins, and all the other tools needed to make a delicious meal. Featuring ceramic tile, travertine, and marble mixed with rustic wood and wrought-iron pot racks or light fixtures, these materials create a warm and homey kitchen, with splashes of color reflecting the Tuscan countryside—the sage green of the olive trees, ocher, honey, blues, and terra-cotta reds—which mingle comfortably alongside the warm patina of aged copper pots.

Sometimes a drying rack hangs above the sink so dishes can be washed and placed just above to dry, and for handy and efficient storage. A clear stone surface for kneading pasta dough, often a table all its own with a marble top, where the dough can be worked, rolled out, and cut into whatever pasta is on for the day. Traditionally, there is a fireplace where meat might be cooked or chestnuts roasted, or bean soup might hang over a fire in a cast-iron kettle. While many delightful scents may emanate from a Tuscan kitchen, a constant is sautéed garlic, the base for so many recipes.

A moka pot, the tiny little Italian percolator, will bubble espresso for mornings or *dopo pranzo* (after lunch) or even *dopo cena* (after dinner).

Most houses have a compost bucket for the organic waste, and many use it for composting in their gardens, while others deliver it regularly to the organic bin in the center of the village. In Kentucky, our chickens get the remainder of our food scraps, which leaves little for me to compost.

When buying a home in Italy, the kitchen will often have no appliances or cupboards. It was strange to see this when we began viewing properties, until we realized it was normal for Italians to remove a kitchen so the new owner could begin from scratch. It's as if there is a general understanding: This room is far too important to be passed on to the next owner. The new owner must make this space his or her own by creating it from scratch, just like the food.

Bring Italy Home

- ⚜ Grow fresh herbs in kitchen pots, inside or outside, depending on the season.

- ⚜ Make a list of your go-to pantry staples to always keep on hand.

- ⚜ Read Carlo Collodi's *The Adventures of Pinocchio*, one of the highest-selling books of all time.

Pesto Sauce

This pesto sauce recipe was given to me by a longtime friend and business partner of my husband, Millard Oakley. While Millard was born and raised in Tennessee, he had a lifelong love for Italian food.

INGREDIENTS

4 cups fresh basil
½ cup pine nuts
½ cup fresh Italian parsley
½ cup olive oil

3 cloves garlic
1 tsp. salt
½ cup Parmesan cheese

DIRECTIONS

Put the basil, pine nuts, parsley, oil, garlic, and salt in a food processor and mix well.

Add the cheese and process more.

You can freeze the pesto sauce in pint or jelly jars for enough to flavor your pasta or pasta salad. You can also put the pesto in ice cube trays, freeze them, then pop the pesto cubes out and put them in a plastic freezer bag in case you want a small amount to flavor soup or vegetables, like carrots or roasted potatoes. Enjoy!

YIELD: 4 to 6 people or makes 4 (8 oz.) jelly jars to freeze

12

L'Orto

{THE VEGETABLE GARDEN}

People who know the garden in which their vegetables have grown and know that the garden is healthy will remember the beauty of the growing plants, perhaps in the dewy first light of morning when gardens are at their best. Such a memory involves itself with the food and is one of the pleasures of eating.

—WENDELL BERRY

When the colorful seed catalog arrives in February, it is a happy proclamation that spring is around the corner. I order my seeds, usually far more than I need, out of pure exuberance at the idea of something green and growing.

Canning and preserving the food we grow connects me to the grandmothers I never knew, and their mothers before them. I like the rhythm of the work, the preparation for winter, the joy of eating my own organic vegetables, and the satisfaction of providing for my family.

After several years of plowing a big garden patch and fighting the gnarly weeds fed by the Kentucky July heat and humidity, I shifted to raised beds, which require seasonal rotation, staggered plantings, and more intentionality. A bonus is the ability to access the garden even if it's raining or muddy.

My gardens feature Roma green beans along with my go-to tomatoes—Romas, Cherokee Purples, and Indiana Red Oxhearts. I also like to plant red and yellow onions and various greens in the spring and fall, and cultivate herbs such as basil, rosemary, sage, mint, and oregano. Jess takes pride in his bed of sweet potatoes and manages the orchard with help from knowledgeable friends.

My father was the gardener in our family during my childhood, and I remember taking little interest in the garden, and as a result, learning little about it. When I had my first real job in Lexington, my employer offered garden plots on the land around the headquarters to anyone interested. After living in the city awhile, I was longing for a connection to my farming roots and happily signed up for a plot. They plowed the land, then tilled it, and made it ready for planting. I purchased a variety of seeds, dreaming of eating all the vegetables photographed so beautifully on the outsides of the seed packets, and spent a Saturday planting my garden. Job done; I left the garden to grow.

Sometime in August, I naively decided to check on my plants to see if something was ready to pick. You can imagine what I came upon. My lovely plot was covered in weeds nearly as tall as me. The poor neglected vegetables didn't have a chance but provided a valuable lesson for me: Gardens need tending. So do relationships, skills, and talents. The other lesson I learned: Start small, master that, then work your way up slowly.

We are usually in Tuscany for parts of the summer, not long enough to grow anything other than herbs, but I do keep basil plants, a few strawberry plants, thyme, oregano, rosemary, and even a couple of lemon trees. I especially love it when the lavender blooms a vivid purple and emanates a sweet and relaxing scent, drawing me along with the butterflies and honeybees.

Our tiny yard also includes two plum trees, a cherry tree, a black fig tree, and a cachi tree, a type of persimmon. Our plum tree is called a *coscia di monaca*, which translates to "nun's thigh." Only in Italy will the shape of a ripe plum be likened to a woman's thigh—and that of a nun, no less. The ripe plums fall to the ground in summer, creating a luxurious purple blanket below.

Our fig tree ripens in the dry summer heat when the sunny days turn the fields from green to flaxen gold and the white roads are dusty from lack of

rain. The unique black figs give Jess no end of pleasure and me no end of angst as he stretches out over the steep bank to grab for the one fig always out of reach.

"When I am an old man, I will remember the taste of these Tuscan figs," he says. In deference to his passion and will, I turn my head and pray when he leans a little too far.

One of my favorite warm-weather walks is to go around the village and peer into every *orto* visible from the street to admire the various vegetables in the beginning of the summer and again when we return at the end of the summer to see how the garden has changed.

Tuscans' gardens feature the all-important tomato in various varieties, nearly always including San Marzano, an elongated Roma often used to make pasta sauce and for salads, though others prefer the Piccadilly tomato or the Datterino for sauce making. Artichokes, fennel, leeks, potatoes, and onions are also regularly featured along with a variety of cool-weather greens like chicory, spinach, and lettuces.

Like me, gardeners in Tuscany focus on canning tomatoes so the sauces can be fresh even in winter. The summer plums and figs are often preserved as well, creating a delicious marmalade for bread and toast.

Our *Old Farmer's Almanac* is a handy reference tool for gardeners and has much to say about when to plant and harvest, among many other things, all connected to the moon phase. This might seem a bit strange, but if the moon controls the tides, it is surely possible.

Italy has its own farmer's almanac, one published for well over two hundred years in Umbria, Tuscany's neighbor to the east. It's called the *Almanacco Barbanera*, named after the eighteenth-century astronomer and philosopher, and still thrives today in Spello, where the foundation is headquartered.

Lemon trees are grown in terra-cotta pots and are often featured in gardens both simple and formal in Tuscany, since they not only provide a fruit used in cooking but are also quite decorative. Since they can't survive the Tuscan winter, the potted trees are brought out in April or May, remaining outside until November when they are moved to a lemon house, or *limonaia*, for the winter. Limonaias are usually a simple shed with light, but in formal gardens they're often a beautiful building that gives the lemons winter protection and provides a summer shelter for parties.

I've often wondered how lemons came to be such an important part of a Tuscan garden if they're not native to the area and obviously can't take the winters. I recently discovered the answer lies in the influence of the Medici family. Building on the work of an earlier ancestor, Grand Duke Cosimo III cultivated over a hundred varieties of citrus in the Medici gardens, and the tradition spread throughout the countryside.

<hr>

Though sometimes the language, cultural, and historical differences are obvious to an American in Italy, a connection exists among gardeners and farmers that transcends communication and culture. When I admire the flower bud of an artichoke, the rich red beauty of a tomato, or the size of a leek, I connect with the gardener over a mutual desire to work the land and bring forth fresh and healthy produce. Without saying it, we share a secret: Dirty hands make happy hearts.

Bring Italy Home

❖ Try growing Italian tomato varieties like San Marzano or Roma. If you don't have space for a garden, grow them in containers.

❖ Consider a dehydrator for a simple way to preserve tomatoes and other fruits.

❖ Read the *Old Farmer's Almanac* for growing tips.

❖ Watch *Spettacolo*, a documentary filmed about the village of Monticchiello.

"Sun-Dried" Tomatoes

Sun-dried tomatoes are delicious additions to pastas and soups. Drying distills the tomato to a flavorful richness very different from the freshness in a garden tomato. Since we have a lot of humidity in our Kentucky climate, the idea of spreading out tomatoes to dry in the sun as they do in Italy doesn't work quite as well. My helper is a dehydrator, which dries tomatoes in less than 24 to 36 hours. You can buy these in various sizes, but the one I currently have is stackable, giving you the option of drying a small or large amount.

INGREDIENTS

**Clean and ripe Roma tomatoes,
  as many as you wish to dry**

DIRECTIONS

Wash the tomatoes, then slice them lengthwise and lay them face up on the dehydrator. You may need to experiment with the temperature, but I find it generally takes around 24 hours and up to 36, depending on the size of the tomatoes, the temperature you set for drying, and how much humidity you have. Monitor the first batch until you figure out the best time and temperature for drying. You don't want them crispy, but rather dried enough that the flavor is distilled.

Once dried, you can put the tomatoes in a jar with olive oil and salt to brine for an aperitivo, or you can freeze them for future use in pastas and soups.

13

Il Ristorante

{THE RESTAURANT}

I'd much rather eat pasta and drink wine than be a size zero.
—SOPHIA LOREN

Creating food from fresh ingredients for the purpose of feeding body and soul with conversation and connection around a table is not only for the home. Food is meant to be shared, and experiencing Italy's many restaurant options is a way to participate. Most tourists will recount a noteworthy restaurant discovered where they were made to feel special, a place they want to return to over and over. The combination of tired travelers, welcoming hosts, and nurturing, delicious food featuring local specialties gives us an emotion about an experience and a place, which leads to an unforgettable memory.

Maybe this is often why we all have such a wonderful time in Italy on short trips—we feel as if we've been in someone's home, and for a short time, a part of someone's family. In a time when family businesses are diminishing, it's delightful to see a family work together in a restaurant, each with their own role, each dancing to practiced and choreographed steps.

For both first- and long-time travelers to Italy, it can often be a bit confusing to understand the differences between the types of dining-out offerings, and especially the idea of breakfast being a pastry and a tiny cup of espresso, often taken standing at the bar. Where's the oatmeal, fruit, granola? Or better, the eggs, sausage, and biscuits?

Beyond breakfast, there are *osterias, trattorias, pizzerias,* and *ristorantes,* along with a whole host of other *rias* with some sort of food-related meaning.

Osteria comes from the Latin word *hospes,* which then transitioned to the ancient French word *hoste* and then into English as "host." Since Italians don't recognize *H* in the alphabet, we get *ostello* (a hostel) or *osteria,* which is traditionally a place that hosts travelers for drinks, meals, and overnight stays. Many osterias these days offer food only and have dropped the overnight stays.

A trattoria will have a standard menu, but there will be another daily menu either listed on a board visible to guests or offered at the table. These are specialties, usually cooked by *nonna* (the grandmother), and it's wise to make a choice from one of those. Trattorias will sometimes offer a "worker's meal" for laborers. This is usually a limited menu with extra portions for a set price, affordable and filling for those who need it most.

The differences between a trattoria and an osteria have melded in modern times, but Italians have a saying defining the original purposes: "A trattoria is where we go to eat and eventually drink, but an osteria is where we go to drink and eventually eat."

In either a trattoria or osteria, you can purchase a bottle of wine, but if you want to live like the locals, ask for the house wine in a *litro* (liter), *mezzo litro* (half liter), or a *quartino,* which is around two glasses of wine.

You can ask for a *bicchiere di vino,* glass of wine, but in a trattoria or osteria there is the option of either a *calice di vino* or a *gottino di vino.* A calice di vino is a glass of wine served in a stemmed glass. A gottino di vino is served in what we might call a juice glass or water glass, no stem and no nonsense. A man coming in alone for a meal to read his newspaper might simply order a gottino di vino, while a couple sharing a meal together might order the more elegant calice di vino.

Both the osteria and the trattoria are more casual than restaurants. It's possible you might need to stand up and retrieve your own forks and knives or help yourself to the antipasti, in some form of self-service.

A restaurant will have a higher level of service and a slightly upgraded atmosphere and menu. Here you will buy wines by the glass or the bottle,

since the quartino and the mezzo litro are not options, but either way, you will always be asked first which type of water you prefer, either still water, called *naturale*, or sparkling water, called *frizzante* or *gasata*.

We currently have one restaurant inside the village walls and it's one of our favorite places to eat. It's called 13 Gobbi, which means "thirteen hunchbacks." The number 13 is considered lucky in Italy, and so are hunchbacks, so it literally translates to something sounding like a roadside saloon in Texas: The Double Lucky. It's owned and run by Albo, his wife, Simonetta, and Matteo. They have a special pasta, which is their version of *cacio e pepe* (cheese and pepper pasta), brought out just before serving to be twirled in a great wheel of aged pecorino cheese. This pasta is creamy and delicious, satisfying both child and adult alike. Combined with Albo's agrumello at the end of the meal, it is an excellent prescription for new arrivals, ensuring a good night's sleep.

When we are without guests, we often enjoy experiencing the osterias and trattorias where all the local workers eat. These are places off the tourist path, maybe in industrial areas, where you will get the traditional Tuscan dishes with no fancy twists. Roasted chicken, wild boar, and tripe will often be on the menu in our area along with seasonal specialties and the local handmade pastas. Table wines in quartinos and saltless Tuscan bread used to make the little shoe for sopping up the sauce. Jess will eat anything and likes all manner of meats, fish, seafood, and organs.

Recently, a friend and villager sang the praises of tripe. I knew it was well beyond my gastronomic ability, but Jess wanted to try it, especially after an Italian friend so heartily recommended it. We found a trattoria in a nearby town, tucked off the beaten path. The owner seemed slightly surly, frowning at our appearance, and frowning even more when we said we didn't have a reservation. While some might be put off at this point, I took it as a good sign this restaurant is not for tourists.

It wasn't long before we were seated at a checked tablecloth, snugged against a dark-paneled wall. I scanned the menu and found one of my go-to dishes: pici all'aglione, a rich garlic-infused tomato sauce creating a flavorful but light dish. Jess spotted tripe on the menu and decided to try it, and when he made his choice, the trattoria owner's face lit up. Good choice, he affirmed, and somehow our status as patrons had gone from wayward tourists to real Tuscans with that one menu selection. We were in the club.

Our dishes arrived and I tucked into mine. Jess, on the other hand, finally met a dish he couldn't stomach. Partly because it was cow's stomach, the lining anyway. He knew this of course, but when the presentation came, it looked every bit like a large circular pasta in tomato sauce, and this made the reality even more harsh. It was not pasta.

He ate a few bites and pushed the rest around on the plate, wishing for an overgrown plant nearby to ditch the remaining bites. When the owner returned, he frowned. *"Qualcosa non va?* Is something wrong?" I rarely see my husband stumble over words. He didn't want to admit he couldn't eat it, but he didn't want to lie either. I watched and waited, curious how he would handle this situation and not one bit tempted to bail him out.

Finally, he resorted to gestures, opening his hands to indicate he was stopping. *"Basta,"* he said, using the Italian expression for "It's enough."

Bring Italy Home

❖ Is there a travel experience you can re-create for family or friends at home through music, special dishes, table decorations, a recipe you can try, or even some spices or canned food items you tuck in your suitcase? Sometimes the planning is as much fun as the event itself, and it's a way to take a memory home and share with others, whether it be from Tuscany or your own special place.

❖ Try some Tuscan wines, a white vermentino or Vernaccia Di San Gimignano, or perhaps go red with a Rosso or Vino Nobile di Montepulciano or across the Val D'Orcia to Montalcino with a Rosso or Brunello di Montalcino and of course the reds from the famous Chianti region.

❖ Read *Where Angels Fear to Tread* by E.M. Forster.

❖ Watch one of Sophia Loren's many movies and enjoy a performance by one of Italy's national treasures.

Cacio e Pepe

Cook in Tuscany, a cooking school based in Montefollonico, provides this *cacio e pepe* recipe so you can savor your own creamy pasta experience at home. This is sure to be a crowd-pleaser for both adults and children.

INGREDIENTS

½ cup butter (just under to equal 100 grams)
½ cup olive oil
1 cup hot water
4 tsp. or more black pepper

⅛ teaspoon salt
4 T. Parmigiano cheese
4 T. pecorino cheese
Freshly cooked pasta

DIRECTIONS

Melt the butter in olive oil on low heat in a deep saucepan.

When the butter is melted, add hot water, pepper, and salt.

Cook the sauce for 1 minute, then add Parmigiano and pecorino and continue cooking for another 2 minutes until the cheese is melted. Add fresh pasta and toss until the pasta is coated with sauce. Serve with a sprinkle of Parmigiano cheese on top.

Recipe courtesy of Cook in Tuscany

YIELD: **4 servings**

14

Generosità e Regali

{GENEROSITY AND GIFTS}

For it is in giving that we receive.
—ST. FRANCIS OF ASSISI

When our house restoration was completed, the first gifts we were given by our Tuscan neighbors and friends were bottles of a traditional local dessert wine called vin santo. This was not something purchased off the alimentari shelf but made by the hands of these friends. Our electrician gifted us a bottle of olive oil, pressed from his own family's recently harvested olives.

Gifts often have certain meanings in Italy, beyond being symbols of generosity and goodwill. Wine represents hospitality and friendship while olive oil signifies good health. Gifts are often given with a great deal of flourish, sometimes accompanied by ribbons and colored paper or even delicate silk flowers, and usually presented with two hands.

We enjoy giving, but we have come to realize it is impossible to outgive our Tuscan friends and neighbors. We have sometimes presented a bottle of wine or even some of my handcrafted goat milk soap to a new friend as a symbol of friendship, only to be surprised within hours by a visit and a bottle of something as a return gift, a way to seal the act of friendship.

This cultural practice carries over into the younger generation. A couple of years ago, Jess befriended a boy in the village who was eager to try out his school-learned English on this Americano. He and Jess have become buddies, and recently, Leo entertained us with some impressive wheelies on his bike. Jess gave him twenty euros as a thank-you for the show he provided to us. "No, Jess," he said, all the while eagerly taking the money. With an encore wheelie, he rode off. Fifteen minutes later, we were back at the house after our walk. The doorbell rang and it was Leo, bringing Jess a Coca-Cola. Friendship sealed.

Aside from a thirteen-year-old's gift of Coca-Cola, nearly every gift we have received has been from the land, and generally made by the hands of the giver. Wine, vin santo, olive oil, digestivi such as mirto or limoncello, a jar of tomato sauce, plum jam, porcini mushrooms or truffles found in the forest. These gifts are treasures, delights to nourish the soul and the body and given with love from the most precious asset we humans have: time.

To create a gift with your own hands is a pleasure surpassing anything purchased. Tuscans seem to live and breathe this maker society as naturally as we might shop for a gift. The offering of something handcrafted is a gift from the very soul of a person. When I share a jar of my canned green beans or tomatoes, this act represents hours of picking, washing, and canning. It is a gift of time, talent, and heart.

Even if you don't make your gift, there is still a way to invest your own time into an offering. *La bella figura* is the Italian idea of "presenting well," whether it be your person, a gift, or even an item you have just sold to someone. The first time I noticed this extra attention to detail was when we bought some paintings for our newly renovated house. There were four small paintings we could have easily laid in the back seat of the car. But that was not possible for the Italian store owners. We patiently waited while each painting was

protected on all four corners, then wrapped carefully in brown paper, then tied off with a colorful silk ribbon. Only then could we depart the store with our purchases.

There is pride in how something leaves the business. So, even if you don't invest your time in making the gift, perhaps the extra attention to detail in the way it is presented will make the gift special and will also serve as an outlet for your creativity.

While gifts are one form of generosity, so also is our time. A long pause to chat on the street, an invitation to our home, or treating someone to lunch or dinner. If we look at generosity as a tree, then hospitality and gifts must be the branches. Acts of generosity have surprising benefits for the giver far beyond a sense of connection and goodwill. Todd Harper, a founder of Generous Giving says, "I've never met an unhappy generous person."

Bring Italy Home

- ⚜ Add a homemade touch to a gift. This can take many forms, from styling a ribbon or making your own wrapping paper to drawing something on the side of a bag or creating your own card.

- ⚜ If you are a maker of something, who might benefit from an unexpected gift?

- ⚜ Watch *A Room with a View*.

- ⚜ Listen to Luciano Pavarotti.

Fig Jam

Fresh figs are a summer staple in Italy, and this is a standard jam made by the locals. It's wonderful served on a charcuterie board, with cheeses, on toasted bread, and it also makes a deligtful gift.

INGREDIENTS

2 lbs. ripe figs

1¾ cups sugar

½ cup water

¼ cup lemon juice

DIRECTIONS

Stem the figs and cut them into smaller pieces, under an inch in size. In a pot, toss the fig pieces together with the sugar. Add the water and lemon juice, turn on the heat, and bring to a boil until the sugar has dissolved. Reduce the heat and simmer until the mixture thickens. Spoon into sterilized hot jars (keep them in a warm oven until ready for the jam), being careful to wipe any jam from the lip of each jar and make sure it is dry so the lid can seal. Place the lids, twist on the bands, then turn the jars upside down for 10 minutes. After 10 minutes, turn the jars upright, and the lids should seal with a pop as the jars cool. If any jars don't seal, they can be stored in the refrigerator for up to three months.

YIELD: **4 (8 oz.) jelly jars, and maybe a bit more for breakfast the next morning.**

15

Artigiani

{THE MAKERS}

Facendo s'impara. We learn as we make.

—ITALIAN PROVERB

Aspire to live quietly, and to mind your own affairs,
and to work with your hands.

—THE APOSTLE PAUL, THE FIRST
LETTER TO THE THESSALONIANS

On one of our early trips to the village during the harvest in October, we were eager to buy new olive oil. We asked a villager to tell us where to go for the best oil and expected her to direct us to one of the local mills. Instead, she pointed down the street and says, "Enzo sells oil, and it is very good." The land behind his house falls steeply to the valley floor below, with no room for an olive grove.

"Where are his trees?"

"Outside the village. He goes every day."

There was no sign on the door promoting the sale of olive oil. We knocked, and hoped we had the right door, feeling a little as if we were trying to make a clandestine transaction. When Enzo answered, we recognized him as the caretaker of one of the properties we viewed when house hunting. He is a compact man with gray hair, his eyes gentle and patient as he waited for Jess to stumble over his Italian, asking if we can buy some oil. He understood enough and motioned us inside.

We followed him through his living space to an office of sorts where every item seemed to have a place. Through another doorway, we stepped down into his cantina, where the oil is stored. He pulled out a tall green bottle and held it under the nozzle of a stainless-steel vat. Bright green liquid streamed into the bottle. Jess praised the oil's color while Enzo accepted the compliment with a grin, a maker proud of his creation. He twisted on the cap and sealed it, no label, no branding. We asked for three more, handed over a modest amount of euros, then walked out of Enzo's house as if we had won a prize.

Halfway up the hill from Enzo's home is Mariella's ceramic shop, housed in a deconsecrated private chapel. Some of her pieces are purely artistic, but most are beautiful platters, dishes, bowls, and cups for the table. This pottery is made in the style of maiolica, a tin-glazed pottery decorated in colors on white background, and is renowned from the Italian Renaissance period. The chapel has workspace in the anterooms on the side where she has large tables for painting the ceramics, a massive kiln for firing the pieces, and a place for shipping finished pieces. Tables line the center of the chapel with samples of plates, art pieces, and grand platters. My Tuscan house is filled with her creations and even my kitchen wall features a tiled art piece she painted of Benedetta's garden.

Farther up from Mariella's ceramic chapel is Mr. Innocenti's cantina. Like Enzo, Mr. Innocenti tends to his vineyards out in the countryside, yet the heart of his operation is here inside the village, where he makes and bottles the wine in two different locations. The large tanks where the grape juice goes for fermentation after harvest are hidden behind nondescript garage-style doors. Inside the cantina, visitors are guided through a mysterious maze of underground passages where the wine is aging in barrels, then into his *vinsantaia*, where his famous vin santo ages in small barrels called *caratelli*, and beyond into another hallway leading outside to a grass terrace with a panoramic view of the Val d'Orcia for tastings.

Mr. Innocenti is beyond retirement age and shows no sign of slowing down. He takes great joy and pride in his work, and his award-winning vin santo has secured his spot as chief judge for the local vin santo festival.

Terra-cotta means "baked earth," and the tradition of creating terra-cotta pots in our area goes back for hundreds of years as typical Sienese craftsmanship. My appreciation for terra-cotta has grown as I learn more about the process, how long it has been practiced, how the makers sign their pots, and how the old creations are strengthened with wires when they crack so the pots can be preserved.

There is also an art to the terra-cotta flooring featured in so many Tuscan homes. When our house was being renovated, we visited a factory just under an hour away on winding country roads. The owner took the time to demonstrate the entire process of making the terra-cotta tile in the form, the gray clay smooth and pliable, then sprinkling some ash on the clay so it would have antique-looking pockmarks after it was fired. Then he popped it from the form and laid it in a line with the other tiles to dry before it would go into the kiln. I could hardly imagine the time it would take to handcraft each tile needed for our downstairs and upstairs floors. Sometimes still, I am filled with wonder at our terra-cotta floors, and think of the many hands that created and laid the herringbone pattern.

Bottega Artigiana del Cuoio is a delightful tiny shop in Pienza where you can watch leather goods being made by owner and artisan Valerio Truffelli with assistance from his wife. The shop smells of leather, a contrast to the scent of pecorino cheese hovering around the entrance of Pienza.

They produce beautiful journals, wallets, belts, and various other leather creations. The shop even has a "Tired Pilgrim's Chair" outside during the day in case you need a rest after a long day of sightseeing. Every time we visit Pienza, I am frequently drawn there to spend a few minutes watching Valerio work the leather and create something beautiful. I nearly always come away with yet another leather journal since a writer can never own enough blank pages.

Anna Porcu is a Pienza-based artisan jewelry designer who handcrafts beautiful jewelry with museum-quality cameos. While she travels to shows all over the world, her work is uniquely Italian, combining the art of the ancient cameo with Italian leather, which gives her pieces a high-fashion look.

Outside of Pienza is Ferro Battuto Biagiotti, a long-standing family business that creates a wide range of attractive and creative wrought-iron pieces to furnish homes with metalwork both functional and beautiful. The forge is in the back of the building, and they welcome visitors to watch the work from a safe distance. The blacksmithing creations are a blend of art and craftsmanship, yet also reflect a great deal of stamina for the heat emanating from the forge and muscle to pound the metal into something beautiful and delicate. Our house features many light fixtures and other items they've created, a sweet reminder of the work, sweat, and artistry invested into each piece.

Mary Lippi is an art restorer and conservationist from Montepulciano. Though she doesn't paint the paintings, she is a master artist at cleaning them, removing the centuries of dust and grime, insect excrement, and other dirt. She repairs and restores the painting and frame to its original glory, an artistry all its own. She has been entrusted with countless works of art created by famous Renaissance painters in Italy, including Caravaggio.

While I have never worked on a Caravaggio painting, nor handcrafted leather, nor painted ceramics, I connect with these makers and understand the spiritual connection existing between humans and handwork. We create handcrafted goat milk soap, the result of a human mixing, pouring, cutting, drying, and boxing the soap. It then goes to another human being, who will use it to clean and moisturize their skin. It is the same with planting, harvesting, and creating canned goods from my summer garden, a therapeutic practice for me.

It's been said before that if you work with your mind, you should rest with your hands. If you work with your hands, rest with your mind. As a writer, I am in my head and on my laptop good chunks of the day, so it is relaxing, even joyful, to pick green beans in the summer, to break them and then can them. Cooking one of my standard soups does the same thing for me, allowing my mind to rest while I chop vegetables and listen to a book. Beyond relaxation, there is deep satisfaction in making something with your hands, especially when it is shared and enjoyed with others.

I could fill a whole book simply featuring the makers and artisans of southern Tuscany, but one of the most mystifying examples came to light when we were restoring our house. Marco, retired firefighter, tree pruner, and jack of many trades, went into our cistern to clean it and came out with photos of

an unbelievable piece of art. He showed me how the cistern—made for the purpose of holding water in a dark, underground place rarely viewed—was created with terra-cotta bricks laid out in a beautiful herringbone pattern. He knew of only one other like it, in the palazzo of the noble family who once owned our property as their former horse stables.

Who creates a piece of art knowing it will rarely be seen? Perhaps someone who honors the work of the ultimate Creator, the One who fashions magnificent beauty in the depths of the ocean.

Bring Italy Home

- ❖ Take a class to learn a skill or craft you are interested in acquiring, such as ceramics, painting, mosaics, knitting, cooking, gardening, or canning.

- ❖ Watch *Dream of Italy* with Kathy McCabe, the PBS series where she often features the makers of Italy.

- ❖ Read *Made in Italy: Strings Attached—Four Seasons of an Italian Violin* by Thomas Walter Kelley.

- ❖ Read *The Shoemaker's Wife* by Adriana Trigiani.

- ❖ Read Laura Morelli's historical fiction books based on the artisans and artists of Italy.

Caprese Skewers

This version of the Italian caprese salad does not include the olive oil or the plated presentation, yet it still has the notable red, white, and green colors representing the Italian flag. Best served in summer when the tomatoes and basil are fresh from the garden. Plan on having an equal amount of each ingredient, enough to create sufficient skewers for the number of people you wish to serve.

INGREDIENTS

Wood skewers, 3 to 4 inches in length
Cherry tomatoes

Fresh, clean basil leaves
Buffalo mozzarella balls

DIRECTIONS

Skewer a cherry tomato, then a basil leaf, and then a mozzarella ball. Plate and serve.

La Camminata e la Passeggiata

{THE WALK}

Walking is man's best medicine.

—HIPPOCRATES

Marco Landucci and his wife were a Sienese noble family who owned extensive lands around Montefollonico two hundred years ago. His wife decided there must be land set aside for public use, thus creating the Parco Tondo by donating 117 acres of land for forest walking around the village. Strangely enough, despite being the one who initiated the gift, her name is unrecorded. While her name may be lost to the ages, the land is not, and abundant trails surround the village, providing endless walks and connections to other trails.

Jess and I regularly set out on these marked trails adjoining the village streets, tramping through peaceful woods, picking our way over stones, scrambling on loose gravel, and pausing when a breathtaking view opens beyond the trees. Our goal is to take one of these walks every day, but even on the days we don't, we log a surprising number of steps moving about the village. While each season holds its own pleasure, spring and early-summer walks are especially delightful with the blooming of yellow *ginestra* on both sides of paths and roads. The garden roses are bursting in a myriad of colors, and the iconic red poppies dot verdant green fields, refreshed with the winter rains and nourished by the gentle spring sun.

⚜

"*La camminata?*" Viviana asks when she sees us at the city gate, tennis shoes laced and ready to go. When we say yes, she asks, "*Dove?* Where?" There are two standard walks around the village, one up to Parco Tondo, which not only means the 117 acres of land but can also mean the walk to the top of it, where cypress trees stand like guarding sentinels in a circle at the very tip of the village hill. Or we might be doing the *giro*, which is a two-mile circular walk on the two roads leading into the village from opposite directions—one the proper entrance to the village, and the other leading to the cemetery road and the *campo sportivo,* or the athletic field.

If we were heading out around six in the evening, then the question might more likely be "*La passeggiata?*" This is a leisurely stroll, often connected to the walk taken around the square or village in the evening before dinner. It's a time to visit with friends before going home for the evening meal, to see and be seen. Whatever time of day, I often see the older gentlemen walking with their hands behind their backs in a slow and measured pace. I tried it one day and discovered the act of connecting my hands behind my back balanced my body as I walked up a hill. This posture also keeps the pace slow and thoughtful rather than hurried.

Some of the best conversations I have had with Jess, family, or friends have taken place while walking and talking. Somehow, not making eye contact can lessen the intensity and emotions of the subject and enable the talker to more freely express thoughts and feelings. Maybe the physical aspects of heart pumping and blood flowing give us a clearer mind in the light of day.

⚜

For those wanting something beyond la passeggiata or la camminata, there is a hike or *escursione,* which can take you from one village to another, either on white gravel roads or on well-marked footpaths. The white gravel roads offer a certain scenic beauty as they meander through vineyards and farms, and footpaths often crisscross in and out of them. On one of our early visits to the area, we parked our car to the side of a gravel road and took a marked trail leading into the woods. The hike took us up and down hills, in and out of forests and pastures, and even led us by a farm where a mysterious white horse wandered freely in an old, abandoned barnyard.

Far below our village, in the Val d'Orcia, there is an old pilgrimage trail called the Via Francigena, which means the road from France. It begins in Canterbury, England, and winds down through France and Switzerland to Rome, and even beyond into Puglia, where a ship can be boarded for the Holy Land. While either Rome or the Holy Land is the ultimate destination, the journey is about what happens along the way, what we learn about God, ourselves, and others, symbolic of our life on earth with heaven as our destination.

Reasons to embark on a pilgrimage may be a desire to see a church or sacred place, a way to let go of worldly possessions and take only the most needed items, enduring physical challenges to increase your dependence on God. It might also be for healing, penance, or forgiveness.

In a day and time of so many distractions, the idea of setting off on a foot journey, being totally dependent on God through the meditation and solitude, encountering other pilgrims on the same road, relying on the hospitality of others for food, drink, and a bed for the night—or at least a friendly campfire—all might sound archaic, but I find it intriguing.

There is a website dedicated to Via Francigena, and I read this leg of the trail near us covers a challenging thirty-three-kilometer section known as Leg 36. It's particularly difficult because the very end of the trail requires the hiker to climb five miles up to Radicofani. Many hikers break up the leg into two parts, spending the night in a town called Gallina, which is a bit more than halfway.

On a recent trip to Italy, I spent the first week on arrival working on this book, gathering pictures and recipes, writing, and since I only had a week with my photographer relative, we were burning the candle at both ends. I knew I wanted to include the pilgrimage trail in this book, so earlier in the week, we found the trailhead out of San Quirico for the Via Francigena and took a few pictures. Walking along the trail for a mile or so gave me an idea.

"What if we do a few miles of the pilgrimage trail?" I mused aloud. Jason, my rock-climbing, tree-pruning, salmon-fishing photographer, heartily agreed. My niece Lea Ann, not a hiker, consented to drive the car so she could pick us up on the trail after five miles or so. Five miles was a reasonable goal. After all, I had not trained for a nearly twenty-three-mile walk and had never tackled such a thing in my life. I once walked fifteen miles in the Cotswolds in England, only because we got to a village and couldn't get a taxi back. My knee swelled and was covered in an ice pack the rest of that evening, and that was years ago.

I regularly walk four miles at home, so I could surely do five miles. There was one problem. My left knee, the same one I had iced all those years ago after the Cotswolds walk, was now bothering me with a strange new discomfort since I made the unwise decision to carry ten heavy coffee-table books up two flights of stairs. I was concerned it was the beginning of a real knee problem, the kind ending with surgery.

We needed a change of pace and fresh air, so we set a day near the end of our week's work. The day promised to be mostly sunny, with the typical spring afternoon threats of a thunderstorm. I found a small backpack, threw in some snacks, sunscreen, a bottle of water, a rain jacket, and carried my walking poles. I took another bottle of water to leave in the car. After all, we were meeting Lea Ann around mile three, so no need to carry so much water.

Jason had a much bigger backpack, likely because his previous experiences taught him to prepare for another person's lack of preparation. How right he was.

Lea Ann dropped us at the trailhead around 7:15 in the morning and off we went. I said a silent prayer in hopes my knee would hold up for a five-mile trek.

We walked and talked, and Jason took photographs. Often, he lagged for a good photo while I plodded ahead and used the solitude for reflection.

Around three miles or more, we met Lea Ann at Bagno Vignoni, then set the next connection point another three or four miles away, which put us well beyond our goal of five. Shortly after getting back on the trail, I drained the last of my water, and realized I forgot to get the other water bottle from the car. Jason still had water, but surely, I could make it to the next meeting point with Lea Ann.

Unfortunately, we missed that meeting point since she couldn't find us. Jason texted her instructions for another stop, another three miles or so beyond. I was getting thirsty, but not desperate, so before I tapped into Jason's water supply, I decided to do what one should do on a pilgrimage trail: I prayed for water.

A couple of miles later, we left the paved road for a meandering gravel road that sliced through a wheat field. Up ahead, workers clattered around on a farmhouse roof, replacing terra-cotta tiles. I trudged past, then glanced back to check on Jason. He was unloading his pack on a picnic table in the yard of the house. It took me a second to realize other hikers were there, filling water bottles from a fountain.

I made a beeline for the water and slaked my thirst before filling up the bottle for the road. We sat at the picnic table where I noticed a cabinet set up with electricity to provide coffee by the cup along with a variety of packaged cookies. Now we were beyond the provision of needs and into desires. I savored every sip of a luxurious morning coffee, then stuffed euros in the offering box.

While relaxing, we chatted with other pilgrims, hailing from Belgium, Germany, and Switzerland. The Belgian couple offered their snacks to us, and we enjoyed a sense of camaraderie, fellow travelers on a long road. It was an unexpected gift, one I nearly missed because I wasn't looking for it.

We met up with Lea Ann at lunchtime when Jason looked at his smartwatch and said, "We're over halfway there."

When he said those words, I realized it was possible to finish.

"Let's keep going." We sealed the plan with a high-five. Then we ate sandwiches, drank more water, and hit the trail. Jason told me his adventure stories, distracting me from the growing hot spots on my feet. I told stories from some of my travels, and in this way, we passed the time.

Storm clouds gathered in the afternoon about fourteen miles into the journey and we felt a smattering of rain. Bolts of lightning flashed in the distance and thunder rumbled. We were hiking in an open field with nowhere to take shelter. We kept going while storms stayed in the distance on both sides of the trail, with nothing more than a breeze and a short sprinkle of rain.

We followed the trail signs placed strategically at any crossroads or fork in the road, indicating two directions, one to Canterbury in England (north) and the other to Rome (south), which was the direction we followed. Around seventeen or eighteen miles into the hike, Lea Ann met us next to the trail and noticed the sign to Rome for the first time.

"Now, am I picking y'all up in Rome?" she asked in earnest. I laughed hilariously, almost uncontrollably, because Radicofani may as well be Rome.

As we placed one foot in front of the other, the tower of Radicofani came into view, and we felt the elevation shift upward. This was undoubtedly the hardest part of the journey mentally. The hot spots were now blisters and my feet hurt with every step. The muscles in my hips felt like tight and painful knots. Strangely enough, my knees were fine. Onward we went, one step in front of the other.

When we finally reached Radicofani, the pilgrimage ended at the church, but that didn't seem like the right place to stop. After looking at the tower across the valley throughout most of the walk, we needed to end our hike there. On we went, up the final hill to the base of the tower. Sadly, when we reached the top, the gate into the parking lot was locked. We pulled the car to the side of the road and took a victory picture with the tower in the background.

After the photo was snapped, the gatekeeper drove out and paused to chastise us for being in the road. Jason explained we had just finished walking twenty-three miles, missed the opening time, and only wanted a moment to take a photo.

"You should have left earlier in the morning!" That statement was followed with another round of fussing at us for being in the road.

As her Fiat moved down the hill, we fell laughing into the car, repeating her words: "We should have left earlier!"

When I finally stopped laughing, I found the second bottle of water in the back seat of the car, never used since water was provided all along the way.

Then I reached down and felt my left knee. It was completely normal. No swelling and no pain. I rolled down the car window and felt the breeze on my face as I pondered my own little pilgrimage miracles, all the way home.

Bring Italy Home

- Park your car in the spot far away from the store, your work, school, or church entrance.

- Plan visits with friends while walking.

- Push yourself to go a little farther than normal, take a harder walk, and climb a higher hill.

- Read *My Brilliant Friend* by Elena Ferrante.

- Watch *The English Patient*.

Elena's Tiramisù (Pick-Me-Up)

My friend Elena and her husband, Simone, are owners of Osmosi, a Michelin-starred restaurant near Montepulciano. Her simple *tiramisù* is my go-to recipe for a light and yummy dessert that serves well all seasons.

INGREDIENTS

3 egg yolks
½ cup brown sugar
2 containers mascarpone cheese
  (500 g. total)

Pavesini cookies (ladyfingers), around 40
1 cup espresso
Unsweetened cocoa powder for dusting

DIRECTIONS

Mix the egg yolks and sugar into a foam. Add the mascarpone cheese and continue mixing until thoroughly incorporated and smooth. Dip the Pavesini cookies in espresso coffee and place on the bottom of a dish. Top with one-third of the cream mixture, then continue adding the espresso-dipped cookies and the cream until you have three layers. Dust the top with cocoa. Refrigerate or serve immediately.

YIELD: 6 to 8 servings

17

La Foresta

{THE FOREST}

*Our village life would stagnate if it were not for
the unexplored forests and meadows which surround it.*
—HENRY DAVID THOREAU

While Kentuckians have a long history of living off the land, going back to the pioneers who carved a path through the wilderness, Tuscans have been living off the land much longer. Every season in Tuscany brings some new treasure to scavenge for in the surrounding woods, from greens and truffles to mushrooms and chestnuts.

Once, on a springtime walk through the Parco Tondo, we saw a woman bent over, snipping plants from the underside of the hill. A scarf was tied around her hair, and she was intent on her work. We watched for a few moments, trying to determine what she was foraging. Finally, Jess called out in Italian to ask.

"*Ortiche*," she said, putting her hand over her eyes and squinting through the sunlight. Nettles. These springtime plants have mean little hairs ready to sting exposed skin. When we first looked at our Tuscan house with the realtor, I inadvertently walked into a patch of nettles and paid for it later in the night when the stinging pain kept me awake. For all their rough exterior, these tiny stinging hairs are easy to remove, and the plant then makes a tasty addition to spring salads. Later, we discovered this woman is a talented local forager. She searches for the best spring varieties of greens and then sells them to restaurants.

Truffle-hunting season can be in the spring or the autumn. The Lagotto Romagnolo is a breed of dogs originating in Italy and used for centuries to hunt truffles. They look a bit like poodles, are smart, loyal, and friendly, and have a keen sense of smell. One of our village friends also uses a Jack Russell terrier to hunt.

While truffles and mushrooms are both the fruiting body of a fungus, mushrooms are fleshy and live above ground while truffles are hard and grow below ground. Truffles generally hide under the roots of chestnut, oak, and hazelnut trees. Some describe the flavor as earthy chocolate, while others detect notes from the parent trees or even garlic and shallots. While the black truffle can be found in spring or autumn, the prized white truffle, *il tartufo bianco*, can only be found in the fall and is often likened to the smell of fermented cheese.

It's nice to think of dogs working in a way they were bred, of man taking something the ground has produced, of hunting something without requiring the loss of life.

⁂

Autumn is also the season of the chestnut harvest on Monte Amiata, just across the valley from us. Festivals are held in villages on the mountain to celebrate these nuts used to make snacks and soups and to flavor pasta.

For many of us, "chestnuts roasting on an open fire" is nothing more than a dreamy line in a famous Christmas carol, because most of us have never experienced roasted chestnuts. The American chestnut trees were almost completely wiped out by disease in the first years of the twentieth century, and the delicious nut, once a prevalent part of the rural diet, was also wiped from our palates.

A number of years ago, we traveled to a cooking school in Pienza, the first time I had ever been to this area of Tuscany I now call home. It was November and we were on our third and last night of the cooking class. We shared the trip with our best friends and travel buddies, Wes and Roni. I had taken a break from the kitchen when my phone buzzed with terrible news for my

friend Roni. Her father had died suddenly in Spain where he lived.

The next hours were a flurry of decisions and restless sleep. We saw them off early the next morning to the Florence airport, then began making our way north to visit Verona and see the town famous for so many things, including the balcony claimed to be the inspiration for *Romeo and Juliet*.

The weather turned cold, and it was spitting snow. We were troubled in our spirits for our friends, and we felt a little forlorn. As we wandered the piazza, cold and shivering, Jess spotted a man selling roasted chestnuts, nestled into paper cones, warmed by a heat lamp. He smiled at two eager customers, even though we were more excited about holding something with heat rather than eating the nuts. With the warm cone of chestnuts in my hand, all my concentration went into inhaling the delightful scent, removing the shells, and then tasting the sweet and buttery soft nuts. All troubles seemed to fall away, and for a few moments, it felt like a heavenly ministration. These jewels of the forest are more than worthy of the famous old carol.

The Italian chestnut trees populate the forested areas in Tuscany and are in groves on the side of Monte Amiata. When autumn arrives and the nuts ripen and fall, they are gathered and sold for roasting and eating over the open fire, or for making soups and sauces. They're even made into a paste and sold in jars for topping bruschetta. I will forever connect the soul-comforting roasted chestnut with Italy.

Our first year in the village, Marco brought us three porcini mushrooms the size of softballs. I had no idea what to do with them, and I was slightly nervous about eating them, since I'd heard too many stories about Appalachian families picking the wrong mushrooms and ending up in the hospital or worse.

After thanking him profusely for the gift, I put them in the refrigerator for a couple of days, eyed them suspiciously, and then finally erred on the side of caution and passed them on to our Italian next-door neighbors. They were delighted.

When Marco brought them around again the second year, we took the plunge and fried up the most delicious bites of meaty mushroom. I found out the name means "little pigs," a name given to them by the ancient Romans, which only endears them to me even more. Now, when autumn rolls around, we eagerly await these little piggies from the forest.

Bring Italy Home

- Learn the names of trees.

- Gather nuts on a family outing, shell them together, then roast and enjoy them.

- Buy chestnuts in the autumn and try roasting them over an open fire.

- Read *Beneath a Scarlet Sky* by Mark Sullivan.

- Watch *Letters to Juliet*.

Fried Porcini Mushrooms

The meaty porcini mushroom makes the perfect one for frying. Depending on the size, one mushroom can easily serve two or more people.

INGREDIENTS

Porcini mushrooms
2 eggs, beaten
1½ cups all-purpose flour mixed
    with salt and pepper to taste

Frying oil of choice
    (peanut, safflower)

DIRECTIONS

Clean the mushrooms with a damp paper towel and cut away the lowest part of the stem (the not-so-pretty part). Slice the mushrooms in half and cut them again into slices of the same thickness, but not too thin. Dredge each slice completely in the beaten egg, then in the flour mixture, then put them into an iron skillet with hot oil. Turn the mushroom slices with a fork and cook until both sides are golden brown. Lay them on a plate covered with paper towels to remove the excess oil. Serve hot.

18

Il Campo

{THE FIELD}

The soil is the great connector of lives, the source and destination of all.
—WENDELL BERRY

As the descendent of a long line of farmers that extends as far back as my genealogy can be traced, I see the land as life-giving for me, and while I appreciate every season, I love the summer best because it is when I can plunge my hands into dirt and grow vegetables, fruit, and flowers.

Here in Tuscany, I sense the same spirit among the inhabitants, but know the roots go even deeper in a land where farmers have been living, surviving, and thriving for many centuries. The Val di Chiana to our northeast is famous for fertile ground, for its rich yield of wine grapes and Chianina beef—large white cows with comically long legs. On the other side of Montefollonico, the Val d'Orcia historically supported farms cultivating wine grapes, olives, grains, fruits, and vegetables but today is best known for pecorino cheese, made from sheep's milk. The farmers in the area speak in almost romantic terms about their wines, olives, and animals, with strong *emozione*, or emotion.

As I write these words, we are in the middle of the Tuscan harvest. It is a sweet time of year in early October with the last days of the grape harvest and the beginning of the olive harvest. It is one of my favorite seasons to be here, to watch with pleasure as the farmers bring in the fruits of their year-long labor. With wine, there is a long time to wait before they can taste the final product, but they know immediately if the harvest is good, whether it has the potential to be a spectacular year or just so-so.

Kentucky is where winemaking began in the United States in 1798, when the Marquis de Lafayette's winemaker, Jean-Jacques Dufour, set out to find the best place for growing grapes. Winemaking thrived there until Prohibition destroyed the industry but has recently made a comeback, and Kentucky is currently the largest producer of wine in the South. However, we are best known for another alcoholic beverage, bourbon whiskey, where 95 percent of all bourbons in the world are made due to the limestone-infused water and availability of good corn. Kentucky has more barrels of bourbon than people. Does Tuscany have more casks of wine than people? I imagine so.

Our local winemaker, Mr. Innocenti, hand-cuts the grapes from his vineyards, the traditional way to harvest the fruit from the vine. Larger vineyards use machines driven between the rows and aggressively attack the vines to capture the grapes. After the grapes are cut, we enjoy watching Mr. Innocenti bring his grapes into the village, tiny load by tiny load, and follow the grapes as they go through the machine to be crushed and made into juice before funneling into the waiting vats for fermentation.

On the heels of the grape harvest come the olives. What makes a superior wine vintage doesn't always make good olives, and one good harvest doesn't guarantee the other.

The traditional method for olive trees is to lean ladders against the trunk, allowing pickers to comb the olive branches gently with rakes, letting the olives fall to a net below the tree. There are also battery-powered twizzle forks called *abbacchiatore*, which vibrate the branches and drop the olives to the net below. Many large farms use an even more violent method whereby machines circle a tree with a net and then shake the trunk of the olive tree, causing all the ripe olives to drop.

Combing the olive trees for olives is a repetitive motion both relaxing and meditative. I wonder if the tree likes it as much as I do, receiving the gentle pull, the loosening of the fruit, the giving up of its year of work, and the freedom to face winter knowing it has done its job for the year. The quiet

combing allows conversation with the other workers, a sweetening of the time spent working, something not possible with the loud drum of machines.

<hr />

At the nearby *frantoio*, or olive mill, loads of olives from local farmers are dropped in crates to be cleaned and crushed, then the oil is extracted and filtered before being bottled. The vivid green oil, pungent and delicious, tickles the back of the throat with its peppery freshness. Local olive oil festivals are held in nearby villages, celebrating the new oil picked green and peppery, with samples displayed at vendor booths for tasting, and bottles ready for purchase.

While we have no investment in these grapes or olives, we can't help but feel a deep sense of satisfaction when the harvest is delivered, despite threats from weather, disease, and blight.

<hr />

The landscape in Tuscany is breathtaking, but I often find my husband wants me to snap pictures of a Tuscan tobacco crop or a particularly large tractor, or even one with treads instead of wheels for the steep slopes. We have taken many photos of hay bales precariously perched on the sides of hills, and placed precisely so they won't roll into the valley below, although some do. We note and ponder the differences between Tuscan and Kentucky farming practices, yet the similarities are strong. We all live by the seasons and the weather.

Though not a part of the harvest, the iconic Tuscan cypress trees lining drives and standing as guards along white gravel roads also serve a purpose. They provide a windbreak for the fields, helping with conservation of the land, in addition to providing an aesthetically pleasing landscape. They are thought to have been brought from the Middle East by the Etruscans, most likely deriving from Syria or Persia. Many of these majestic trees were planted as memorials to the fallen soldiers of World War I, to remember the young men, gone too early.

The Avignonesi Winery conducted a fascinating experiment many years ago to determine the ideal spacing to plant grapevines. The research was carried out in a field with the vines near the center planted closest to each other in a circle, and then successive plantings farther away in concentric circles beyond. Over the years, the project showed the vines planted nearer to the center, but not at the center, performed the best. The vines needed to be close to each other but also to have a bit of space to thrive. Maybe humans mirror creation in more ways than we can even imagine.

Bring Italy Home

- ❖ Support local farmers and farmers' markets.

- ❖ Grow your own herbs and vegetables, or try container plants if space doesn't allow for a garden.

- ❖ Take trips into the countryside as a reminder of what the land does for our well-being and nourishment.

- ❖ Read *My Italian Bulldozer* by Alexander McCall Smith.

- ❖ Watch the film *Only You*.

Giovanna's Roasted Eggplant (Melanzane)

INGREDIENTS

Two medium-size eggplants
Olive oil
½ cup parsley leaves
2 garlic cloves

1½ cups dried breadcrumbs
1 tsp. salt (optional)
½ tsp. black pepper (optional)

DIRECTIONS

Preheat the oven to 350°F.

Slice the eggplant ¼ inch thick. Drizzle a bit of olive oil in a pan and place the eggplant slices in the pan, being careful the slices don't cover each other. Drizzle or brush a small amount of the olive oil on top.

Chop the parsley and garlic very fine. Mix with the breadcrumbs. Add the salt and pepper, if desired. Cover the eggplant generously with the breadcrumb mixture to make a crust.

Add a small amount of olive oil on top of the breadcrumb mixture.

Roast the eggplant until the breadcrumbs become golden, around 8 to 10 minutes.

YIELD: 6 servings

19

Riposo
{REST}

Painting is concerned with all the 10 attributes of sight; which are:
Darkness, Light, Solidity and Colour, Form and Position, Distance
and Propinquity, Motion and Rest.

—LEONARDO DA VINCI

The afternoon sun blazes on a Tuscan summer day. Grass, dry and crunchy, seems almost to be crying out for water. The chalky white dust swirls from the *strada bianca* as we make our way home from a long lunch in a nearby medieval town. The walk from the car to the village takes every ounce of energy in the heat, and once inside the cool stone walls of our home, there is only one thing to do: rest.

The window shutters are closed, keeping out the heat, and the dark room is surprisingly cool without air-conditioning. Jess takes a couch and I take the bed, and soon we are fast asleep in the land of dreams. It's an hour before I stir and find Jess still sleeping. This never happens at home, this luxurious hour of restoration. Yet here in Tuscany, it is as natural as planting red geraniums in terra-cotta pots.

While the afternoon rest period is common all over Italy, it's often difficult to observe in the cities, where fatigued travelers push themselves, panting and breathless, from Rome to Florence to Venice, historic sites melding into one antiquated blur.

Off the beaten path, the authentic countryside demands this rest, especially in summer when the brilliant and unrelenting sun depletes energy and even the smallest tasks take on mammoth proportions.

There is great wisdom in the whole of society shutting down and saying, "Rest now." It is still a sacred time observed by most shopkeepers, offices, banks, and other places of business not owned by large multinational companies. Work is done in the morning and late afternoon, but midday is for food, family, and rest.

The *riposo* is rooted in the agricultural schedule, based on the intense heat of the hot-weather days when most of the outdoor work is done. This is not unlike my own agricultural roots, which link to a time when the largest meal was eaten at lunch and went by the name *dinner*.

The noon dinner bell was rung outside my grandparents' kitchen door to call the farmworkers in for the noonday meal. It was a large daily feast, with a meat and vegetable sides, mashed potatoes and cream gravy, biscuits or sourdough bread, sweet tea, and always meringue pie for dessert. After dinner, they went outside and sat on chairs or on the ground under the shade of trees, talking, smoking pipes, telling stories and jokes. My sister remembers lots of laughter, the men playing with the dog, and the water jug being refilled for the afternoon work. An hour was given to this time to eat and rest, and then back to the field they would go until around five or six in the evening.

Under the Mediterranean sun, the habit of eating a large lunch, usually with wine, and then taking a rest in the most extreme heat of the day, extends the afternoon break. They often work well past what Americans might consider the end of the day, sometimes until seven in the evening. In the afternoon, when one o'clock comes, my house cleaner will stop whatever she is doing so she can walk to her home in the village, eat a sandwich, and take a nap. She usually returns around two thirty or three. She would never consider pushing through to finish, or downing a protein bar in place of lunch, even if only an hour remained. I appreciate her lunchtime departure because it gives me a chance to enjoy my own lunch break while she is gone.

Post-lunch tends to be my errand-running time in Kentucky, so it took a few times arriving at a closed shop here in Tuscany before I came to accept

this new schedule. Each shop sets their own rest hours as well, so one might open again at three, another three thirty, and the others at four or four thirty.

Beyond shops, I've learned there is a cultural understanding regarding the sacredness of the lunch period. Visits to your neighbors are not made between one and three in the afternoon, unless you have been invited to lunch or have made some special arrangement to meet a bit before three. At first, these new hours of functioning seemed a bit restricting to me, like a time budget. Once again, freedom is found within these boundaries.

Riposo is an invitation for many things beyond taking a nap. It's a time to pause for a moment and process the morning before rushing into the afternoon and evening. The days I find the most challenging are the days I must go from one meeting to the next, with no time to process or organize from the previous meeting. When I call our Italian electrician about a need we have at the house, he always says, "Let me organize and I will message you with a time I can come." I like this idea of downtime to "organize" or mentally prepare.

In a country specializing in engines that power Maseratis, Lamborghinis, and Ferraris, there is understanding about calibration, the process of creating optimal engine performance with minimal fuel consumption. To recalibrate is to adjust when things are off, to get back to optimized performance. Perhaps our bodies need the same, and daily rest in the afternoon is a way to give our bodies and minds the chance to recalibrate so we can give our best.

Not only is the afternoon rest a part of daily life, but the Sabbath rest is also a part of weekly life. *Buona Domenica* is often used as a greeting on Sunday mornings, implying Sunday, or Domenica, is a different day than all the others, a day set apart for a different rhythm. Sundays in Italy mean attending church, enjoying a long and lingering lunch with family, then savoring a rest period. Sunday evenings tend to be a time to connect with friends or visit during la passeggiata.

My grandfather always said, "Work on Sunday, come hard on Monday." He meant Mondays will be an especially hard day if you don't go into it rested from the previous week. Sabbath is a gift, and our bodies need this buffer day to rest, prepare, and be restored after a prior week of work and before tackling another one.

In the Jewish tradition, there is the idea of weekly sabbatical for the land, but also an entire rest period for the ground through Jubilee every fifty years. The modern idea of crop rotation practiced in our own culture is a return to this important idea of periodic rest. In livestock agriculture, as well, thoughtful periods of rest improve not just the health of pasture and livestock but productivity too. On our cow farm, our son grazes the herds regeneratively, alternating periods in which the cows intensely graze a small section of pasture, harvesting the nutritious grasses with their sharp teeth at the same time they fertilize it with their waste, stirring up microorganisms with their trampling hooves. The stimulated pastures respond with vigor during the long periods of rest following each grazing.

Most of my life, I have operated on the idea of work hard and rest later. The rest is a reward for all the hard work. A friend in ministry once rattled me when she said rest was often God's preparation for what was coming rather than what had already been.

There were times when God prepared me for such seasons. I remember well the year I turned fifty. As a nod to the Jewish Jubilee, I decided to let my garden rest for the first time since I had moved to the farm. No planting, no harvesting, and no canning. A summer rest for the land and for me. Shortly after I made this decision, my father-in-law suffered an accident and spent six weeks in critical care before finally succumbing to his injuries. I was so thankful I didn't have the needs of a garden on top of the mental and emotional distress of that time.

There are seasons when it is especially important to build in a few extra minutes to recognize where you are and recalibrate yourself by allowing time to think and mentally shelve your books.

One day at the end of October, I had two Italian friends share with me how exhausted they were. Both work in shops serving tourists, and the time from May to October is particularly busy. Within hours, both women recounted something that exacerbated the exhaustion, but I know those incidents were only the proverbial straw. It's the end of the season for them, and six months of an intense workload have taken their toll. More is needed than a few days at the sea. What is needed is the slow pace of winter, the time for shorter days and longer nights, to rest, recuperate, and recover, so by spring of next year, the smiles are wider and the eyes are brighter. Seasons are God's way of giving us the rhythm of rest.

For most of my adult life, winter was a season to be endured with the gray days, whipping wind, and a sleeping monochromatic creation outside. More recently, I've learned to stop resisting and enduring, and to start valuing the gift of rest winter gives us. Strangely enough, I have gained two seasons this way, since the joy of autumn was diminished with the dread of winter following. Now I relax into the beauty of fall, and when winter comes, I enjoy every day, appreciating the slower pace, the cozy nights by the fire, and the time to read and reflect.

Winters in Tuscany are not as harsh, and temperatures generally hover at the freezing mark or above. Snows generally don't linger on the ground long, if there is snow, and instead the winter is marked by rain and fog. Many restaurants will take a few weeks to a month off during February and into early March, a necessary break after serving guests and tourists during the intense periods. Restaurant owners are more relaxed, the tourist sites less crowded, and we are reminded of how Italy might have been long ago, years before our world became so accessible and small.

Winter is the Sabbath of seasons, a gift of much-needed rest.

Bring Italy Home

❖ Carve out an extra half hour after lunch to use as time to reorganize and recalibrate. Use the time to process through the events of the morning, make notes, schedule a meeting, or follow up on phone calls.

❖ Practice taking a Sabbath, one day a week set aside for rest.

❖ Read the book *24/6* by Matthew Sleeth.

❖ Listen to the music of Ludovico Einaudi.

Ribollita

If winter is a season of Sabbath, I can think of no better recipe than the comforting goodness of ribollita soup. *Ribollita* translated means "reboiled," and it is a wonderful way of using stale bread for a delicious soup that becomes even thicker and creamier after a day or two. After tasting the combination of veggies, beans, and greens and the starchy goodness of bread, it is easy to see how this hearty soup became a staple of the Tuscan peasant diet and is still popular today. As with most soups, you can vary the ingredients to your taste, but here is a recipe I use.

INGREDIENTS

½ cup extra-virgin olive oil
1 large yellow onion, diced
3 large carrots, peeled and diced
3 celery stalks, diced
1 (28 oz.) can whole, peeled
   tomatoes, undrained
2 (15 oz.) cans cannellini beans
1 tsp. dried oregano
1 tsp. sea salt

½ tsp. black pepper
1 bunch black kale
1 (32 oz.) carton organic chicken or
   vegetable broth (use as needed)
8 pieces dry day-old or toasted Italian
   bread
Parmesan cheese, grated for garnish
Olive oil for garnish

DIRECTIONS

Heat the olive oil in a large pot or Dutch oven over medium heat. Add the diced onion, carrot, and celery. Sauté until the onions are translucent, less than 10 minutes. Stir in the tomatoes, the beans, and their cooking liquid. Season with the oregano, salt, and pepper. Add the kale and chicken or vegetable broth as needed to bring the mixture to a soup consistency. Bring to a boil, then reduce heat to simmer for 1 hour. Add the pieces of stale or toasted bread to the mixture and stir. Serve with a slice of toasted bread and a bit of parmesan cheese grated on top, along with a splash of olive oil.

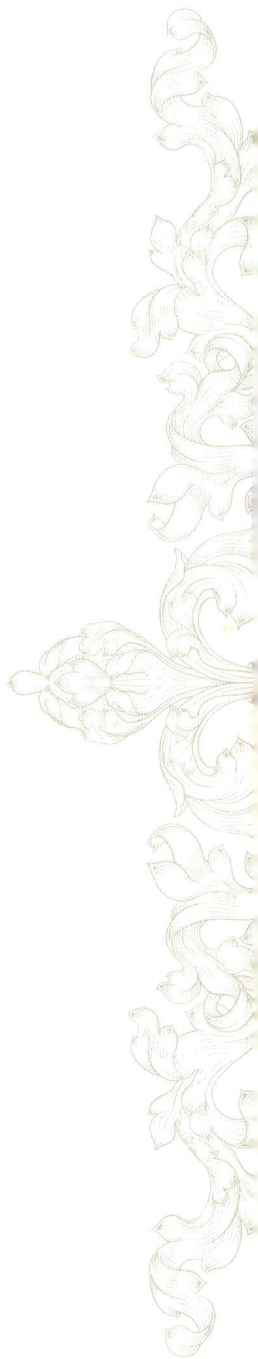

20

Vacanze e Giorni Santi

{HOLIDAYS AND HOLY DAYS}

Speak to the people of Israel and say to them, These are the appointed feasts of the LORD that you shall proclaim as holy convocations; they are my appointed feasts.

—THE PROPHET MOSES, THE BOOK OF LEVITICUS

Holidays began as holy days, and in Italy, the meshing of the two is even more evident, as the spiritual and secular life are combined. While different cities and regions may have additional feasts or celebration days, there are several celebrated all over Italy. Observing the various holidays over the years, or at least parts of the celebrations, is a reminder to grasp the joy and sacred simplicity of each.

The longest celebration is Christmas, which begins on December 8 with *L'Immacolata Concezione*, or the Immaculate Conception of Mary. Christmas lights are hung, and *presepi*, the elaborate Nativity scenes that originated with artisans in Naples, are on display and open for viewing.

After the festivities begin on December 8, there is *Vigilia di Natale*, or Christmas Eve, and then *Natale*, Christmas Day.

Much of work stops in Italy around December 22 or so, depending on the year, until after Epiphany on January 6, very unlike our approximate week or so of Christmas celebrations. This is a time to be with family, to feast, to rest, to travel around and view the *presepi* in other villages, to enjoy the osteria and trattoria with friends and family.

We traditionally spend Christmas on our Kentucky farm, but just this last year, we left the day after to celebrate the wedding of our daughter. The air was festive, there were delicious Tuscan Christmas cookies in the alimentari called *cavallucci*, featuring walnuts, candied peels, and spices. Lights were on display, a Christmas tree stood in the piazza decorated by the school children, and the presepe was open for visitors.

New Year's Eve is celebrated much like our holiday at home, and our house made a good viewing spot for all the fireworks to be seen across the Val di Chiana, but I'll admit, we were all in bed before the show began. It's called the *Notte di San Silvestro*, or the *Vigilia di Capodanno*. Red is the traditional clothing color for New Year's Eve, representing prosperity.

While some of our family had already returned home, we celebrated *Capodanno*, or New Year's Day, with lunch at a local restaurant. After all the family left, I stayed on for a few more days, tying up some loose ends before traveling home. On *Epifania*, or Epiphany, the last day of Christmas, I accepted the invitation of some friends to join them for dinner in Pienza. While there, we experienced firsthand the popular folklore of La Befana, a sort of witchlike woman who was invited by the wise men to come with them on their journey and bring gifts to the Christ child. After an initial refusal because she was too busy with housework, she then tries to follow them but is unable to catch up and find the baby Jesus. Instead, she distributes her gifts to other children. As we finished our meal, two Befanas walked in, dressed in their witchy clothing and with fake witchy noses, exhausted from all their efforts to distribute gifts to children. It made a fun and festive end to a season of celebration, not only the birth of Christ but also our daughter's wedding.

Another major holy day and holiday is Easter Sunday, or *Pasqua*. This is the first Sunday after the paschal full moon, which is the full moon occurring on or after the March or spring equinox. Christians the world over celebrate

the resurrection of Christ when the tomb was found empty. A specialty food item found in the alimentari during this time is the dove-shaped Easter cake called the *colomba pasquale*. The cake is not too sweet and very light, and flavored with candied fruit. Easter Monday, *Pasquetta*, is a time to gather with family and friends to enjoy the beginning of spring. This is usually celebrated with Easter eggs, chocolate, and outdoor dining.

After Christmas, the next grand holy day and holiday must be August 15, or *Ferragosto*—holy because it is Assumption Day, when Catholics believe Mary, the mother of Jesus, was taken up into heaven at the end of her earthly life. It's also a public holiday and originates from the festival of Emperor Augustus, who created a day of rest after weeks of hard agricultural labor. August in general has been the month for Italians to take vacation, but the two weeks from August 15 to the end of August are primed for Italians to flee the cities for the beach or mountains. Many restaurants and other businesses close during this time so the owners can enjoy their own seaside break.

The most memorable Ferragosto we ever experienced was when we enjoyed it like locals the summer our Tuscan house was finished. The village hosted watermelon races and various competitions between the four neighborhood quarters with a grand dinner in the evening. The street was closed, and tables were set up, creating one long table down the main street. Just a few years before, I had longed for a seat at this table, and finally, we were invited to join. Two of my sisters were with us and one brother-in-law (Earl the rabbit). It was a joyful evening, with multiple courses and conversation with new friends, and a lovely way to celebrate the first August in our village home.

Though Halloween is now becoming popular in Italy, the main November holiday is All Saints' Day on November 1, *Tutti i Santi* or *Ognissanti*. All Saints' Day is when many Italians return to the villages where they were born to lay flowers on the graves of their ancestors and give thanks.

Life in the village is often marked by feast days and saint days, as special Masses are offered, processionals are followed, and the village streets are decorated with beautiful flowers.

Within those rhythms are the daily bells ringing at certain times, calling villagers to prayer or to Mass. The first bells of the day toll at eight for morning prayers, and noon is a call for midday prayers. At four thirty and five, the bells remind locals it's time for daily Mass. At seven in the evening, they ring for the Ave Maria, a prayer to Mary, and at eight, they ring a final time as an evening call for the liturgy of Vespers, the evening prayers. The bells are beautiful reminders of the spiritual life of the village and serve another purpose. When a member of the community dies, a bell tolls three times if it's a woman, and two times if it's a man. The village is made aware someone in the community has passed on, and if it is a man or woman.

Just as life is full of feasts, celebrations, and holy days, so it is with hardships, trials, and tribulations. There is no greater reminder of this than a walk down the hillside to Montefollonico's cemetery. At the entrance to the cemetery road is a marker with a skull on it, a stark memorial to the destiny we all share.

A long and shady lane leads back to the cemetery, enclosed by an iron fence. A wall of white marble vaults goes down the length of the cemetery on the left side, and it joins a wall of vaults in the back, creating a walled garden. Graves are in rows on the ground on both sides of a center aisle, many adorned with perennial flowers, or decorative rocks, while some are simple mounds of dirt from recent burials.

More vaults are steps down on the right since the land falls away there on the side of the hill. These village people lived on a hill and are now buried on a hill. While some of the wealthier villagers have their names carved in stone at the top of family chapels, others have simple graves without vaults. Prosperity in life affords some a more elaborate grave, yet death comes to all. Each grave represents the story of a person's life, the comedies and the tragedies, the covert and the overt, the gains and the losses. Their short time on earth over, now they live on in eternity while the shell goes to dust, no matter their status in life.

Bring Italy Home

- ⚜ What are steps you can take to bring the sacred simplicity back into your holidays that are holy days?

- ⚜ If you like the idea of presepe, consider creating your own Bethlehem scene each Christmas. Add new pieces every year and make it a family affair.

- ⚜ Read *Catherine of Siena* by Sigrid Undset.

- ⚜ Watch the 1955 Catholic classic Christmas movie, popular in Italy, called *Miracle of Marcelino*.

- ⚜ Listen to music by Andrea Bocelli.

Adelina's Pan dei Santi

This traditional Italian fruit bread is usually eaten around the time of All Saints' Day on November 1.

INGREDIENTS

Just under 1 cup dark raisins
Vin santo (to cover the raisins)
1 cup walnut pieces
1 packet active yeast
½ cup warm water + ½ tsp. sugar
3¼ cups all-purpose flour

¼ cup sugar
1 tsp. salt
½ tsp. ground pepper
¼ cup extra virgin olive oil
1 egg yolk, beaten

DIRECTIONS

Soak raisins in vin santo for at least 30 minutes or until they have fully plumped. These are the "saints"!

Toast walnuts in a pan with a drizzle of olive oil.

Stir the yeast into the combined warm water and sugar and allow to dissolve according to packet directions.

In a mixing bowl or an electric mixer, combine dry ingredients of flour, sugar, salt, and pepper. Mix well together. Add olive oil slowly and mix in.

Add the yeast mixture a little at a time. Continue to mix all the ingredients.

Drain raisins, then add nuts and raisins to mixture and mix by hand so nuts and raisins remain whole.

Work the dough with your hands until it has absorbed all the ingredients. More flour can be added if needed. The dough needs to be firm enough to form a round loaf of bread.

Cover with plastic wrap and then place a cloth on top. Let rise in a warm place for 3 hours. (You can let it rise overnight.)

After the dough has risen, split and form two smaller round loaves. Place on a baking sheet. Brush the top with beaten egg yolk. Make the cross with a knife, about a half inch deep, enough so it will be visible after baking.

Leave 20 minutes to rest while the oven preheats to 350°F.

Bake for 20 minutes or until the top looks golden.

Remove from oven, let cool, cut, and serve.

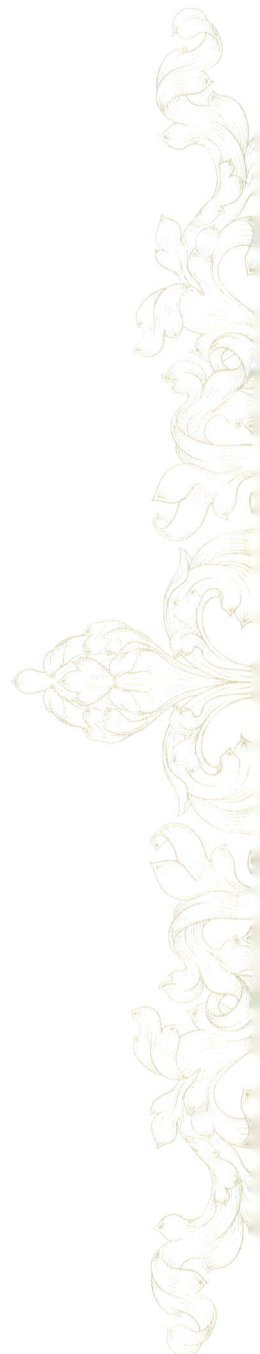

21

Scoperta

{DISCOVERY}

Unexpected wonders happen, not on schedule, or when you expect or want them to happen, but if you keep hanging around, they do happen.
—WENDELL BERRY

Though I could park the car and stay for days on end inside our tiny village, one of our joys is to set off in the morning for some vague destination, to enjoy a day out with no itinerary other than to return home by bedtime. *La gita* is the name for this day trip in Italian, and often when we are asked where we are going, it's the simplest way to answer.

Once, we drove toward the great mountain in our area, a dormant volcano called Monte Amiata, to see a mountainside town called Santa Fiora where we observed an entire block of the village that had been destroyed during World War II and was left as an open piazza in memory of the many people who died on the spot in the bombing. As students of World War II, we find evidence of the war all over this area if we look. After reading about this and soaking in some silent moments to honor what happened, we wandered around the village until we discovered a delicious restaurant. Just the kind we like best, where all the patrons are Italian, and the menu is simple, rustic, and local food. After lunch, we stopped in a clothing shop where cashmere can be procured at half the price of our department stores.

On the trail of more World War II sites, we once explored the tragic village of Civitella in Val di Chiana with our British friends, where the Resistance killed two German soldiers and was paid back with the execution of 149 villagers, including two priests. The entire village was set aflame. It seems impossible in this peaceful and tranquil country that such atrocities of war could happen, but such is the history of this beautiful place.

We sometimes take swimsuits and towels to discover one of the many thermal baths tucked into forests and accessed by winding dirt trails. We often pack tennis shoes in case we discover a hike or need to walk through weeds to find an Etruscan tomb.

For less nature and more cobblestone discoveries, there are the wine villages of Montepulciano and Montalcino, Pienza (the cheese village), the villages of the Val d'Orcia, including Monticchiello, San Quirico d'Orcia, Castiglione d'Orcia, Montisi, Castelmuzio, Trequanda, Bagno Vignoni, Radicofani, and many others. Then there are the Etruscan villages of Sarteano and Chiusi, the larger towns of Cortona and Siena, Assisi, Arezzo, and of course Florence—and so many beautiful villages in between.

We originally thought we would use this Italy home as a jumping-off spot to see other parts of Europe. We've since discovered there is so much to see within a short drive that it's hard to leave the village for anything more than a daytime discovery trip.

After coming to the village for over ten years, we have barely scratched the surface. A new road to go down, a new section of the valley to explore, a new hike to take. This realization has me thinking a bit about my own country roads in Kentucky, and it spurs me to set aside some time for exploration in both places. To allow myself to be surprised and delighted by what might be found. To be gloriously lost for a day, phone turned off and an open road ahead. After all, as J.R.R. Tolkien once said, "Not all those who wander are lost."

Bring Italy Home

- ⚜ Drive down a road you've never been on before.

- ⚜ Take a day trip and explore surrounding towns.

- ⚜ Read the book *War in Val d'Orcia* by Iris Origo.

- ⚜ Listen to *Kimberly's Italy*, a travel podcast.

Peach Crostata

The picture you see here was made by my friend Elena at Osmosi Restaurant and this is based on her recipe. You can also use jam for the filling if time or season prevents you from using fresh fruit.

INGREDIENTS

Crust
3 egg yolks
½ cup powdered sugar
1¾ cups all-purpose flour
11 T. butter (1 stick + 3 T.), room
   temperature, cut up

Filling
4 cups cooked, peeled, and
   sliced peaches
Sugar to taste

DIRECTIONS

Preheat the oven to 350°F.

Knead the crust ingredients quickly until well blended. Split the dough into two equal amounts. Roll out half for the crostata base and place it in the bottom of an 8-inch springform pan.

Drain excess liquid from the peaches, and mix with the sugar. Add the fruit filling atop the pastry, and then top with the other half of the dough, rolled out.

Bake for a minimum of 25 to 30 minutes, or until the crust is cooked through and the top golden.

YIELD: 6 to 8 servings

A Final Word

{AND ONE MORE SWEET FOR THE END}

Yesterday, I ran into my next-door neighbors, Fausto and Viviana. In Viviana's rapid-fire eighty-plus-year-old Tuscan-accented Italian, she told me a light was on in my garden. Sure enough, a light had been left on all day, wasting electricity and serving no purpose. I was grateful for the watchfulness.

Hours later, we were halfway through a bowl of pasta and a tomato salad when the doorbell rang. It was our other next-door neighbor, Trevor, delivering two slices of peach torte made by their inn cook. His wife, Julia, recounted to me how days earlier we had delivered a pot of soup to them just as the neighbor on their other side had given them some homemade bread. Neither of us knew of course, and Trevor had no way of timing the torte delivery just as we were finishing our pasta, but such is the way of village life.

These are just a few of the many things I have grown to love about being in a small village so close to neighbors. Despite our love of the village as it is today, among the locals whose families have lived here for many generations there is a gentle longing for their own youth and how things were back then.

"You should have known the village then," our friend Franco says, wistful. He tells us there was once a factory for making wool sweaters, one that employed many in the village—most interesting since the village was founded by monks who made wool, and the village itself is named after wool makers.

I have had these same feelings about my own small-town roots, since we work to preserve the history of old buildings while also creating new space for local businesses. If we long too much for the past, we can't embrace the now, but there is also the balance of honoring and preserving while renovating and creating. These moments of reflection are important reminders of the community lost, yet they also challenge us to embrace the present moment through all the many ways we can experience the community longed for in days of old: a lingering conversation, a long meal, a last chat because we have margin in our schedule.

Even though we discovered the wonderful aspects of village life by planting roots in foreign soil, it's not necessary to cross an ocean to bring Italy home. Your own village life can be created and enhanced right where you are.

Giovanna's Whipped Ricotta Dessert

Giovanna says the success of this dessert depends on the quality of the ricotta. It needs to be fresh and soft, not dry. Ricotta is made from sheep's milk, so if you can source this directly from a producer, the quality can be ensured. Or you can make your own.

INGREDIENTS

3 cups ricotta (figure about ½ cup
  or 100 g. per person)
3 T. white sugar

Pine nuts
Honey

DIRECTIONS

Whip the ricotta and add sugar to desired sweetness (this may be more or less than the 3 tablespoons recommended). Lightly toast the pine nuts in a dry pan. Put the whipped ricotta in a small dessert dish and top with a sprinkle of toasted pine nuts and a drizzle of honey.

YIELD: 6 servings

Glossary

abbracci	hugs
acqua frizzante **or** *gasata*	carbonated water
acqua naturale	still mineral water
aglione	a type of elephant garlic
agrumello	a liqueur traditionally made with oranges, mandarins, and lemons
alimentari	small grocery market
Almanacco Barbanera	the Italian farmer's almanac
apericena	a spread of small appetizers abundant enough to satisfy as dinner; a new word for a newer idea of a cross between aperitivo and dinner
aperitivo	predinner drink; (pl.) *aperitivi*
arrivederci	goodbye, formal
artigiani	the makers
baci	kisses
basilico	basil
basta	enough
bentornata (o)	welcome back; (pl.) *bentornati*
bicchiere di vino	glass of wine
biscotti	cookies, twice cooked
buona domenica	good Sunday
buona notte	good night
buona sera	good evening
buongiorno	good day
cacio e pepe	cheese and pepper pasta
caffè corretto	corrected coffee, an espresso with liqueur
calice di vino	stemmed glass of wine
cantina	a room or cellar, often underground, used to store wine
cantucci	crunchy almond biscotti, usually paired with vin santo

Capodanno	New Year's Day, January 1
cappuccino	an espresso-based coffee drink with steamed milk foam
caratelli	the small wooden barrels used to age vin santo
cavallucci	Tuscan Christmas cookies with walnuts, candied peels, and spices
cena	dinner
che bello	that's nice
che brutto	that's bad
Chianina	a breed of cow used for beef in Tuscany
ciao	hello and goodbye, used informally
Cinta Senese	a breed of pigs used for pork
cognato	brother-in-law
colomba pasquale	dove-shaped Easter cake
coniglio	rabbit
connessione	connection
contorno	side dishes to accompany the meat course; (pl.) *contorni*
contrada	neighborhood or quarter; (pl.) *contrade*
cornetto con crema	croissant-shaped pastry with yellow cream filling
coscia di monaca	a nun's thigh, referencing the name of a plum
crete senesi	a rocky gray gravel landscape feature of the Val d'Orcia
crostata	a baked pie or tart, usually with fruit or jam
cucina povera	poor kitchen; a diet based on peasant food
dieci	ten
digestivo	a liqueur that can be made from a variety of berries, fruits, roots, herbs, and nuts with purported medicinal qualities that aid the digestion; (pl.) *digestivi*
dolce	dessert
domani	tomorrow
dopo	after
è la vita	it's life
enoteca	a place where wine is stored and displayed for sale or tasting
Epifania	Epiphany, the last day of Christmas, January 6, commemorating the arrival of the three magi to see the Christ child
escursione	excursion; a tour, hike, or daytime adventure

fare la scarpetta	to make the "little shoe" with bread for cleaning up the sauce on the plate
Ferragosto	Assumption Day, celebrated on August 15, when Catholics believe Mary, the mother of Jesus, was taken up into heaven at the end of her earthly life; also, a public holiday as a time of rest for agricultural workers
frantoio	olive mill
fullones	Latin for those who worked and washed wool
gelateria	an ice cream shop
generosità	generosity
giorni santi	holy days
giro	circular
gottino di vino	small tumbler-style glass of wine
grissini	thin and crunchy breadsticks
il campo	the field
il cibo	the food
il conto, per favore	the check, please
il tartufo bianco	white truffle
il tartufo nero	black truffle
il tempo	time
La Befana	a sort of witchlike woman who was invited by the wise men to come with them on their journey and bring gifts to the Christ child, but refused, and then later changed her mind
la bella figura	the beautiful figure or to present well
la camminata	the walk
la casa	the house, the home
la cucina	the kitchen
la digestione	the digestion
la foresta	the forest
la gita	day trip
la passeggiata	a traditional evening stroll in the town center by the residents
Lagotto Romagnolo	a breed of dogs originating in Italy and used for centuries to hunt truffles
Pasqua	Easter Sunday
Pasquetta	Easter Monday
la moka	a small coffee percolator for espresso

la tavola	the table
L'Immacolata Concezione	December 8, the Immaculate Conception, the beginning of Christmas for Italians
limonaia	the lemon house, a place to store lemon trees in the winter
l'insalata mista	mixed salad
l'insalata verde	green salad
litro	liter
l'orto	the vegetable garden
mamma	mama
mattina	morning
melanzane	eggplant
mezzo litro	half a liter of wine, served in casual restaurants
mirto	a digestivo made with myrtle plant berries
Montanini	inhabitants of Montefollonico
Natale	Christmas, the birth of Christ, December 25
non buono	not so nice; (pl.) *buoni*
nonna	grandmother
Notte di San Silvestro	the night of Saint Sylvester, a pope who died on New Year's Eve
Ognissanti	All Saints' Day, November 1, also called *Tutti i Santi*
ortiche	nettles, picked in the spring and used in salads
osteria	a casual tavern-style restaurant with traditional dishes
pan dei santi	holy bread, a traditional fruit bread made for All Saints' Day
panzanella	a chopped summer salad made with stale bread, onions, and tomatoes
Parco Tondo	literally "round park," just outside Montefollonico (proper: *Parco il Tondo*)
persiane	louvered shutters
pesto	a sauce made with a base of basil, garlic, and oil
piacere	pleased, often used as a shortened version of "pleased to meet you"
pici	hand-rolled pasta from the Tuscan peasant diet in the shape of a thick spaghetti
pizzeria	a restaurant serving pizza
pomodoro	tomato

pranzo	lunch
presepe	elaborate Nativity scenes that originated with artisans in Naples and are typically on display and open for viewing; (pl.) *presepi*
primo	the first dish, usually pasta; (pl.) *primi*
prosecco	a lower-alcohol sparkling wine
quando	when
quartino di vino	around two glasses of wine, usually served in casual restaurants
regali	gifts
ribollita	literally, reboiled; a Tuscan stew made with stale bread, tomatoes, and vegetables
riposo	rest
ristorante	restaurant
rosmarino	rosemary
saluti	greetings
salve	hello
salvia	sage
scuretti	louvered shutters
secondo	the second dish, usually meat or fish; (pl.) *secondi*
strada bianca	white gravel roads
tagliatelle	a flat, ribbon-shaped pasta
tiramisù	pick-me-up; also, the name for a dessert with mascarpone, espresso, and Pavesini cookies
trattoria	a casual restaurant with a focus on daily dishes, freshly prepared
undici	eleven
Val di Chiana	the Chiana Valley
Val d'Orcia	the Orcia River Valley, which is below Mount Amiata
Via Francigena	the pilgrimage trail that begins in Canterbury and goes through France and Italy, ending in Rome
vacanze	vacation or holidays
vi aspettiamo	we are waiting for you
vicino	near or neighbor
vin santo	holy wine, the sweet wine that is made from dried grapes and paired with cantucci or taken as a digestivo
vinsantaia	the room where vin santo is aged in small barrels

Sources

While I experienced the Via Francigena firsthand, the website was incredibly helpful in providing more detailed information post-hike regarding routes, specifically the one we took from San Quirico to Radicofani (see www.viefrancigene.org/en/).

Let's Eat Italy!: Everything You Want to Know About Your Favorite Cuisine, by François-Régis Gaudry, was an extremely good resource for understanding food in Italy by regions. It was helpful in confirming some of the basic foods the Tuscan diet is based on and explaining the cucina povera.

The Italian farmer's almanac can be accessed online, as well as information on visiting the foundation and gardens (www.barbanera.it).

A History of Wine in America by Thomas Pinney is a resource that contains information about Jean-Jacques Dufour and the Kentucky origins of the commercial wine industry in America. It is available online as part of the UC Press E-Books Collection, 1982–2004.

Any inaccuracies are mine alone.

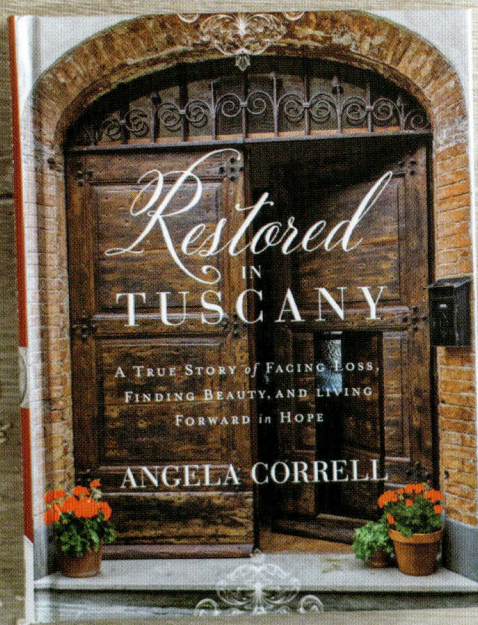

Restoring a Villa, Transforming a Life

Acknowledgments

Jess, as always, for tending to my emotional and physical nourishment during extended writing sessions, for listening to ideas and giving feedback, for supporting and encouraging.

Alessio Capitoni at 6 PM Studio, Montepulciano, for providing many of the Italian pictures in season as they happened.

Jason Asa McKinley of Stanford, Kentucky, for the beautiful cover, for capturing all the extra things we needed to round out the project, and for being my hiking partner on the Via Francigena.

Gabe Osborne and FSNB, for capturing photos during gardening and canning season in Kentucky.

MeDisProject Photography for several beautiful scenes.

John O'Malley, for capturing the amazing Ferragosto table.

Emma Sleeth, my always-faithful editor, for viewing an earlier-than-normal draft to help me give this one some legs.

Beth Dotson Brown, who serves as a gracious and insightful early reader of every manuscript, along with Adrienne Correll and Jan Rawlinson for giving the book a final polish.

Eva Andreucci, for providing accurate historical information about the founding of Montefollonico.

Fulvio Tortora and Geraldine Molinaro, for editing the Italian.

Preston Correll, for keeping me on track with the verbiage for regenerative agriculture.

Tim and Jan Rawlinson, for answering questions and sharing stories as full-time residents.

Fausto Duchini, Rossana Caldi, and Marco Piochi, who through our regular dinners provide great insight into what the village used to be like.

Federica Romani, for help in answering questions so I can describe accurately my observations of village life. Federica, along with her mother, Adelina, and her sister, Laura Romani, for providing recipes.

Andrea Tonini, for providing history and being a great resource for recipes as well.

Carolina Vitolo and Giovanna Fadda for providing recipes.

Linda Meyers with Cook in Tuscany and Coleen Kirnen with Tuscan Women Cook for providing recipes.

Jan Rawlinson and Amy Hines for testing recipes.

The Bar Sport, for creating delicious cappuccinos and the perfect Aperol spritz.

A word about a faithful furry friend who helped me with all five books to date but did not live to see this one completed: Madeline (Maddie) sat beside me and comforted me as I typed, thought, edited, revised, and agonized. I firmly believe God brought me down Knob Lick Road one fateful November morning in 2009 at the same time she nibbled on roadkill. When I placed that little flea-bitten and bedraggled dog in my car, I knew immediately she belonged to me. Fourteen years later, she left us on another November morning, and so I was forced to finish this book without my honorary coauthor. In memory of Maddie and in great gratitude to God for providing such a wondrous little gift, exactly what we both needed.

About the Author

Angela Correll lives on a farm with her husband, Jess, and is the author of *Restored in Tuscany: A True Story of Facing Loss, Finding Beauty, and Living Forward in Hope*, along with a trilogy of novels with stories set in her native Kentucky and her adopted home of Italy. She is cofounder of Wilderness Road Hospitality and enjoys renovation and design for the purpose of hospitality, both in Kentucky and Tuscany. She takes grateful pleasure in traveling and gardening, long walks and long talks, coffee and stories.

For tips on traveling to Italy, recipes, and hospitality updates, sign up for Angela's newsletter at **www.angelacorrell.com**.